THE GOLDEN DAY

The
Golden Day

A *Study in American* *Experience and Culture*

LEWIS MUMFORD

BONI AND LIVERIGHT
Publishers
NEW YORK   MCMXXVI

NOTE

THIS book rounds out the study of American life begun in Sticks and Stones. Where in the first book I used architecture as an index of our civilization, in The Golden Day I have treated imaginative literature and philosophy as a key to our culture. Civilization and culture, the material fact and the spiritual form, are not exclusive terms; for one is never found without at least a vestige of the other: and I need not, I trust, apologize because here and there the themes of the two books interpenetrate.

The substance of this book was delivered in a series of lectures on The Development of American Culture before a group of European and American students at Geneva, in August, 1925. These lectures were given at the invitation of the Geneva Federation; and I gratefully record my debt to Mr. and Mrs. Alfred Zimmern for their constant understanding and sympathy. Without the numerous explorations Mr. Van Wyck Brooks has made, it would have been impossible to make the connected study I have here attempted; and without Mr. J. E. Spingarn's criticism of the final draft of the manuscript more than one page would have been the poorer. The first chapter appeared in *The American Mercury*.

LEWIS MUMFORD.

CONTENTS

Heaven always bears some proportion to earth.

EMERSON.

CHAPTER ONE

THE ORIGINS OF THE AMERICAN MIND

I

THE settlement of America had its origins in the unsettlement of Europe. America came into existence when the European was already so distant in mind from the ancient ideas and ways of his birthplace, that the whole span of the Atlantic did not materially widen the gulf. The dissociation, the displacement, and finally, the disintegration of European culture became most apparent in the New World: but the process itself began in Europe, and the interests that eventually dominated the American scene all had their origin in the Old World.

The Protestant, the inventor, the politician, the explorer, the restless delocalized man—all these types appeared in Europe before they rallied together to form the composite American. If we can understand the forces that produced them, we shall fathom the origins of the American mind. The settlement of the Atlantic seaboard was the culmination of one process, the breakup of medieval culture, and the beginning of another. If the disintegration went farthest in America, the processes of renewal have, at intervals, been most active in the new country; and it is for the beginnings of a genuine culture, rather than for its relentless exploitation of materials, that the American adventure has been significant. To mark the points at which the culture of the Old World broke down, and to discover in what places a new one has arisen are the two poles of this study. Something of value disappeared with the colonization of America. Why did it disappear? Something of value was created. How did that come about? If I do not fully answer these questions, I purpose, at least, to put them a little more sharply, by tracing them to their historic beginnings, and by putting them in their social context.

II

In the Thirteenth Century the European heritage of medieval culture was still intact. By the end of the Seventeenth it had become only a heap of fragments, and men showed, in their actions if not by their professions, that it no longer had a hold over their minds. What had happened?

If one tries to sum up the world as it appeared to the contemporaries of Thomas Aquinas or Dante one is conscious of two main facts. The physical earth was bounded by a narrow strip of seas: it was limited: while above and beyond it stretched the golden canopy of heaven, infinite in all its invitations and promises. The medieval culture lived in the dream of eternity: within that dream, the visible world of cities and castles and caravans was little more than the forestage on which the prologue was spoken. The drama itself did not properly open until the curtains of Death rang down, to destroy the illusion of life and to introduce the main scene of the drama, in heaven itself. During the Middle Ages the visible world was definite and secure. The occupations of men were defined, their degree of excellence described, and their privileges and duties, though not without struggle, were set down. Over the daily life lay a whole tissue of meanings, derived from the Christian belief in eternity: the notion that existence was not a biological activity but a period of moral probation, the notion of an intermediate hierarchy of human beings that connected the lowest sinner with the august Ruler of Heaven, the idea that life was significant only on condition that it was prolonged, in beatitude or in despair, into the next world. The beliefs and symbols of the Christian Church had guided men, and partly modified their activities, for roughly a thousand years. Then, one by one, they began to crack; one by one they ceased to be "real" or interesting; and gradually the dream that held them all together started to dissolve. When the process ceased, the united order of Christendom had become an array of independent and sovereign States, and the Church itself had divided up into a host of repellent sects.

At what point did medieval culture begin to break down? The current answer to this, "With the Renaissance," is merely an evasion. When did it finally cease to exist? The answer is that a good part of it is still operative and has mingled with the customs and ideas that have succeeded it. But one can, perhaps, give an arbitrary beginning and an arbitrary end to the whole process. One may say that the first hint of change came in the Thirteenth Century, with the ringing of the bells, and that medieval culture ceased to dominate and direct the European community when it turned its back upon contemporary experience and failed at last to absorb the meanings of that experience, or to modify its nature. The Church's inability to control usury; her failure to reckon in time with the Protestant criticism of her internal administration; the unreadiness of the scholastics to adapt their methods to the new interests and criteria of science; the failure to prevent the absorption of the free cities, the feudal estates, and the monasteries by the central government—these are some of the stigmata of the decline. It is impossible to give a date to all of them; but it is pretty clear that by the end of the Seventeenth Century one or another had come to pass in every part of Europe. In countries like England, which were therefore "advanced," all of them had come to pass.

It is fairly easy to follow the general succession of events. First, the bells tolled, and the idea of time, or rather, temporality, resumed its hold over men's minds. All over Europe, beginning in the Thirteenth Century, the townsman erected campaniles and belfries, to record the passing hour. Immersed in traffic or handicraft, proud of his city or his guild, the citizen began to forget his awful fate in eternity; instead, he noted the succession of the minutes, and planned to make what he could of them. It was an innocent enjoyment, this regular tolling of the hour, but it had important consequences. Ingenious workmen in Italy and Southern Germany invented clocks, rigorous mechanical clocks: they adapted the principle of the woodman's lathe and applied it to metal. Here was the beginning of the exact arts. The craftsman began by measuring time; presently he could measure millimeters, too, and with the knowledge and technique introduced by the clockmaker, he was ready to make the telescope, the microscope, the theodolite—all of them instruments of a new order of spatial exploration and measurement.

The interests in time and space advanced side by side. In the Fifteenth Century the mapmakers devised new means of measuring and charting the earth's surface, and scarcely a generation before Columbus's voyages they began to cover their maps with imaginary lines of latitude and longitude. As soon as the mariner could calculate his position in time and space, the whole ocean was open to him; and henceforward even ordinary men, without the special skill and courage of a Marco Polo or a Leif Ericsson, could travel to distant lands. So time and space took possession of the European's mind. Why dream of heaven or eternity, while the world was still so wide, and each new tract that was opened up promised, if not riches, novelty, and if not novelty, well, a new place to breathe in? So the bells tolled, and the ships set sail. Secure in his newly acquired knowledge, the European traveled outward in space, and, losing that sense of the immediate present which went with his old belief in eternity, he traveled backward and forward in time. An interest in archæology and in utopias characterizes the Renaissance. They provided images of purely earthly realizations in past and future: ancient Syracuse and The City of the Sun were equally credible.

The fall of Constantinople and the diffusion of Greek literature had not, perhaps, such a formative influence on this change as the historian once thought. But they accompanied it, and the image of historic Greece and Rome gave the mind a temporary dwelling-place. Plainly, the knowledge which once held it so firmly, the convictions that the good Christian once bought so cheaply and cheerfully, no longer sufficed: if they were not altogether thrown aside, the humanists began, with the aid of classic literature, to fill up the spaces they had left open. The European turned aside from his traditional cathedrals and began to build according to Vitruvius. He took a pagan interest in the human body, too, and Leonardo's St. John was so lost to Christianity that he became Bacchus without changing a feature. The Virgin herself lost her old sanctity. Presto! the Child disappeared, the responsibilities of motherhood were gone, and she was now Venus. What had St. Thomas Aquinas to say about theology? One could read the Phædo. What had Aristotle to say about natural history? Leonardo, unaided, discovered fossils in the Tuscan hills and inferred that the ocean was once there. Simple peasants might cling to the Virgin, ask for the intercession of the saints, and kneel before the cross; but these images and ideas had lost their hold upon the more acute minds of Europe. They had broken, these intellectual adventurers, outside the tight little world of Here and Eternity: they were interested in Yonder and Yesterday; and since eternity was a long way off and we'll "be damnably moldy a hundred years hence," they accepted tomorrow as a substitute.

There were some who found it hard to shake off the medieval dream in its entirety; so they retained the dream and abandoned all the gracious practices that enthroned it in the daily life. As Protestants, they rejected the outcome of historic Christianity, but not its inception. They believed in the Eucharist, but they did not enjoy paintings of the Last Supper. They believed in the Virgin Mary, but they were not softened by the humanity of Her motherhood. They read, voraciously, the literature of the Ancient Jews, and the legends of that sect which grew up by the shores of Galilee, but, using their private judgment and taking the bare words as the sum and substance of their religion, they forgot the interpretations from the early Fathers to St. Thomas which refined that literature and melted it into a comprehensible whole. When the Protestant renounced justification by works, he included under works all the arts which had flourished in the medieval church and created an independent realm of beauty and magnificence. What remained of the faith was perhaps intensified during the first few generations of the Protestant espousal—one cannot doubt the original intensity and vitality of the protest—but alas! so little remained!

In the bareness of the Protestant cathedral of Geneva one has the beginnings of that hard barracks architecture which formed the stone-tenements of Seventeenth Century Edinburgh, set a pattern for the austere meeting-houses of New England, and finally deteriorated into the miserable shanties that line Main Street. The meagerness of the Protestant ritual began that general starvation of the spirit which finally breaks out, after long repression, in the absurd jamborees of Odd Fellows, Elks, Wood-

men, and kindred fraternities. In short, all that
was once made manifest in a Chartres, a Strasbourg,
or a Durham minister, and in the mass, the pageant,
the art gallery, the theater—all this the Protestant
bleached out into the bare abstraction of the printed
word. Did he suffer any hardship in moving to the
New World? None at all. All that he wanted of
the Old World he carried within the covers of a
book. Fortunately for the original Protestants,
that book was a whole literature; in this, at least,
it differed from the later protestant canons, per-
petrated by Joseph Smith or Mrs. Mary Baker
Eddy. Unfortunately, however, the practices of
a civilized society cannot be put between two black
covers. So, in many respects, Protestant society
ceased to be civilized.

III

Our critical eyes are usually a little dimmed by
the great release of energy during the early Renaissance: we forget that it quickly spent itself. For
a little while the great humanists, such as More,
Erasmus, Scaliger, and Rabelais, created a new
home for the spirit out of the fragments of the past,
and the new thoughts were cemented together by the

old habits of medieval civilization, which persisted among the peasants and the craftsmen, long after they had been undermined in the Church and the palace.

The revival of classic culture, however, did not give men any new power of command over the workaday routine of life, for the very ability to reënter the past and have commerce with its great minds implied leisure and scholarship. Thus the great bulk of the community had no direct part in the revival, and if the tailor or the tinker abandoned the established church, it was only to espouse that segment called Protestantism. Tailors and tinkers, almost by definition, could *not* be humanists. Moreover, beyond a certain point, humanism did not make connections with the new experience of the Columbuses and the Newtons any better than did the medieval culture. If the criticism of the pagan scholars released a good many minds from Catholic theology, it did not orient them toward what was "new" and "practical" and "coming." The Renaissance was not, therefore, the launching out of a new epoch: it simply witnessed the breakdown and disruption of the existing science, myth, and fable. When the Royal Society was founded in London in the middle of the Seventeenth Century the humanities were deliberately excluded. "Science" was indifferent to them.

Once the European, indeed, had abandoned the dream of medieval theology, he could not live very long on the memory of a classic culture: that, too, lost its meaning; that, too, failed to make connections with his new experiences in time and space. Leaving both behind him, he turned to what seemed to him a hard and patent reality: the external world. The old symbols, the old ways of living, had become a blank. Instead of them, he took refuge in abstractions, and reduced the rich actuality of things to a bare description of matter and motion. Along this path went the early scientists, or natural philosophers. By mathematical analysis and experiment, they extracted from the complicated totality of everyday experience just those phenomena which could be observed, measured, generalized, and, if necessary, repeated. Applying this exact methodology, they learned to predict more accurately the movements of the heavenly bodies, to describe more precisely the fall of a stone and the flight of a bullet, to determine the carrying load of a bridge, or the composition of a fragment of "matter." Rule, authority, precedent, general consent—these things were all subordinate in scientific procedure to the

methods of observation and mathematical analysis:
weighing, measuring, timing, decomposing, isolating
—all operations that led to results.

At last knowledge could be tested and practice
reformed; and if the scientists themselves were
usually too busy to see the upshot of their investigations, one who stood on the sidelines, Francis Bacon,
was quick to announce their conclusion: science
tended to the relief of man's estate.

With the aid of this new procedure, the external
world was quickly reduced to a semblance of order.
But the meanings created by science did not lead
into the core of human life: they applied only to
"matter," and if they touched upon life at all, it
was through a post-mortem analysis, or by following Descartes and arbitrarily treating the human
organism as if it were automatic and externally
determined under all conditions. For the scientists,
these new abstractions were full of meaning and
very helpful; they tunneled through whole continents of knowledge. For the great run of men,
however, science had no meaning for itself; it transferred meaning from the creature proper to his
estate, considered as an independent and external
realm. In short, except to the scientist, the only
consequences of science were practical ones. A new

view of the universe developed, naturally, but it was accepted less because of any innate credibility than because it was accompanied by so many cogent proofs of science's power. Philosophy, religion, art, none of these activities had ever baked any bread: science was ready, not merely to bake the bread, but increase the yield of the wheat, grind the flour and eliminate the baker. Even the plain man could appreciate consequences of this order. Seeing was believing. By the middle of the Seventeenth Century all the implications of the process had been imaginatively grasped. In 1661 Glanvill wrote:

"I doubt not posterity will find many things that are now but rumors, verified into practical realities. It may be that, some ages hence, a voyage to the Southern tracts, yea, possibly to the moon, will not be more strange than one to America. To them that come after us, it may be as ordinary to buy a pair of wings to fly to remotest regions, as now a pair of boots to ride a journey; and to confer at the distance of the Indies by sympathetic conveyances may be as usual in future times as by literary correspondence. The restoration of gray hairs to juvenility, and renewing the exhausted marrow, may at length be effected without a miracle; and the turning of the now comparatively desert world into a Paradise may not improbably be effected from late agriculture."

IV

The process of abstraction began in the theology of Protestantism as an attempt to isolate, deform, and remove historic connections; it became habitual in the mental operations of the physical scientist; and it was carried over into other departments.

The extended use of money, to replace barter and service, likewise began during this same period of disintegration. Need I emphasize that in their origin Protestantism, physical science, and finance were all liberating influences? They took the place of habits and institutions which, plainly, were moribund, being incapable of renewal from within. Need I also emphasize the close historic inter-connection of the three things? We must not raise our eyebrows when we discover that a scientist like Newton in Seventeenth Century England, or Rittenhouse, in Eighteenth Century America, became master of the mint, nor must we pass by, as a quaint coincidence, the fact that Geneva is celebrated both as the home of Jean Calvin and as the great center of watches and clocks. These connections are not mystical nor factitious. The new financial order was a direct out-growth of the new theological and scientific views. First came a mechanical method of measuring time: then a method of measuring space: finally, in money, men began more widely to apply an abstract way of measuring power, and in money they achieved a calculus for all human activity.

This financial system of measurement released the European from his old sense of social and economic limitations. No glutton can eat a hundred pheasants; no drunkard can drink a hundred bottles of wine at a sitting; and if any one schemed to have so much food and wine brought to his table daily, he would be mad. Once he could exchange the potential pheasants and Burgundy for marks or thalers, he could direct the labor of his neighbors, and achieve the place of an aristocrat without being to the manner born. Economic activity ceased to deal with the tangible realities of the medieval world —land and corn and houses and universities and cities. It was transformed into the pursuit of an abstraction—money. Tangible goods were only a means to this supreme end. When some incipient Rotarian finally coined the phrase, "Time is money," he expressed philosophically the equivalence of two ideas which could not possibly be combined, even in thought, so long as money meant houses, food, pictures, and time meant only what it does in Bergson's *durée*, that is, the succession of organic experiences.

Does all this seem very remote from the common life? On the contrary, it goes to the roots of every activity. The difference between historical periods, as the late T. E. Hulme pointed out, is a difference between the categories of their thought. If we have got on the trail of their essential categories, we have a thread which will lead outward into even remote departments of life. The fact is that from the Seventeenth Century onward, almost every field was invaded by this process of abstraction. The people not affected were either survivals from an older epoch, like the orthodox Jews and Roman Catholics in theology, or the humanists in literature, or they were initiators, working through to a new order—men like Lamarck, Wordsworth, Goethe, Comte.

Last and most plainly of all, the disintegration of medieval culture became apparent in politics. Just as "matter," when examined by the physicist is abstracted from the esthetic matrix of our experience, so the "individual" was abstracted by the political

philosopher of the new order from the bosom of
human society. He ceased, this individual, to maintain his omnipresent relations with city, family,
household, club, college, guild, and office: he became
the new unit of political society. Having abstracted
this purely conceptual person in thought—he had,
of course, no more actual existence than an angel or
a cherub—the great problem of political thinking
in the Eighteenth Century became: How shall we
restore him to society?—for somehow we always find
man, as Rousseau grimly said, in chains, that is, in
relations with other human beings. The solution
that Rousseau and the dominant schools of the time
offered was ingenious: each individual is endowed
with natural rights, and he votes these political
rights into society, as the shareholder votes his
economic rights into a trading corporation. This
principle of consent was necessary to the well-being
of a civil society; and assent was achieved, in free
political states, through the operation of the ballot,
and the delivery of the general will by a parliament.

The doctrine broke the weakening chain of historical continuity in Europe. It challenged the
vested interests; it was ready to declare the existing corporations bankrupt; it was prepared to wipe

away the traditional associations and nets of privileges which maintained the clergy, the nobility, the guilds. On its destructive side, the movement for political liberty, like that for free contract, free association, and free investigation, was sane and reasonable; for the abuses of the past were genuine and the grievances usually had more than a small touch of justice. We must not, however, be blind to the consequences of all these displacements and dissociations. Perhaps the briefest way of characterizing them is to say that they made America inevitable. To those who were engaged in political criticism, it seemed that a genuine political order had been created in the setting up of free institutions; but we can see now that the process was an inevitable bit of surgery, rather than the beginning of a more organic form of political association. By 1852 Henry James, Sr., was keen enough to see what had happened: "Democracy," he observed, "is not so much a new form of political life as a dissolution and disorganization of the old forms. It is simply a resolution of government into the hands of the people, a taking down of that which has before existed, and a recommitment of it to its original sources, but it is by no means the substitution of anything else in its place."

v

Now we begin to see a little more clearly the state
of mind out of which the great migrations to the
New World became possible. The physical causes
have been dwelt on often enough; it is important to
recognize that a cultural necessity was at work at
the same time. The old culture of the Middle Ages
had broken down; the old heritage lingered on only
in the "backward" and "unprogressive" countries
like Italy and Spain, which drifted outside the main
currents of the European mind. Men's interests became externalized; externalized and abstract. They
fixed their attention on some narrow aspect of experience, and they pushed that to the limit. Intelligent people were forced to choose between the fossilized shell of an old and complete culture, and the
new culture, which in origin was thin, partial, abstract, and deliberately indifferent to man's proper
interests. Choosing the second, our Europeans
already had one foot in America. Let them suffer
persecution, let the times get hard, let them fall out
with their governments, let them dream of worldly
success—and they will come swarming over the
ocean. The groups that had most completely shaken
off the old symbolisms were those that were most

ready for the American adventure: they turned themselves easily to the mastery of the external environment. To them matter alone mattered.

The ultimate results of this disintegration of European culture did not come out, in America, until the Nineteenth Century. But its immediate consequence became visible, step by step, in the first hundred and fifty years or so of the American settlement. Between the landing of the first colonists in Massachusetts, the New Netherlands, Virginia and Maryland, and the first thin trickle of hunters that passed over the Alleghanies, beginning figuratively with Daniel Boone in 1775, the communities of the Atlantic seaboard were outposts of Europe: they carried their own moral and intellectual climate with them.

During this period, the limitations in the thought of the intellectual classes had not yet wrought themselves out into defects and malformations in the community itself: the house, the town, the farm were still modeled after patterns formed in Europe. It was not a great age, perhaps, but it had found its form. Walking through the lanes of Boston, or passing over the wide lawns to a manor house in Maryland, one would have had no sense of a great wilderness beckoning in the beyond. To tell the truth, the wilderness did not beckon: these solid townsmen, these freeholders, these planters, were content with their civil habits; and if they thought of expansion, it was only over the ocean, in search of Palladian designs for their houses, or of tea and sperm-oil for their personal comfort. On the surface, people lived as they had lived in Europe for many a year.

In the first century of colonization, this life left scarcely any deposit in the mind. There was no literature but a handful of verses, no music except the hymn or some surviving Elizabethan ballad, no ideas except those that circled around the dogmas of Protestantism. But, with the Eighteenth Century, these American communities stepped fully into the sphere of European ideas, and there was an American equivalent for every new European type. It is amusing to follow the leading biographies of the time. Distinguished American figures step onto the stage, in turn, as if the Muse of History had prepared their entrances and exits. Their arrangement is almost diagrammatic: they form a résumé of the European mind. In fact, these Edwardses and Franklins seem scarcely living characters: they were Protestantism, Science, Finance, Politics.

The first on the stage was Jonathan Edwards: he figured in American thought as the last great expos-

itor of Calvinism. Edwards wrote like a man in a
trance, who at bottom is aware that he is talking
nonsense; for he was in love with beauty of the soul,
like Plato before him, and it was only because he
was caught in the premises of determinism that, with
a heavy conscience, he followed his dire train of
thought to its destination. After Edwards, Protes-
tantanism lost its intellectual backbone. It developed into the bloodless Unitarianism of the early
Nineteenth Century, which is a sort of humanism
without courage, or it got caught in orgies of re-
vivalism, and, under the name of evangelical Christianity, threw itself under the hoofs of more than
one muddy satyr. There were great Protestant
preachers after Edwards, no doubt: but the triumph
of a Channing or a Beecher rested upon personal
qualities; and they no longer drew their thoughts
from any deep well of conviction.

All the habits that Protestantism developed, its
emphasis upon industry, upon self-help, upon thrift,
upon the evils of "idleness" and "pleasure," upon
the worldliness and wickedness of the arts, were so
many gratuitous contributions to the industrial
revolution. When Professor Morse, the inventor of
the telegraph, was still a painter, traveling in Italy,
he recorded in one of his letters the animus that

pervaded his religious creed: the testimony loses
nothing by being a little belated. "I looked around
the church," he wrote, "to ascertain what was the
effect upon the multitude assembled. . . . Everything around them, instead of aiding devotion, was
entirely calculated to destroy it. The imagination
was addressed by every avenue; music and painting
pressed into the service of—not religion but the
contrary—led the mind away from the contempla-
tion of all that is practical in religion to the charms
of mere sense. No instruction was imparted; none
ever seems to be intended."

It is but a short step from this attitude to hiring
revivalist mountebanks to promote factory morale;
nor are these thoughts far from that fine combination of commercial zeal and pious effort which char-
acterize such auxiliaries as the Y. M. C. A. The
fictions of poetry and the delusions of feeling were
the bugbears of Gradgrind, Bounderby, and
M'Choakumchild in Dickens's classic picture of industrialism: for the shapes and images they called
forth made those which were familiar to the Protestant mind a little dreary and futile. It was not
merely that Protestantism and science had killed the
old symbols: they must prevent new ones from devel-
oping: they must abolish the contemplative attitude

in which art and myth grow up, and create new forms for man's activities. Hence the fury of effort by which the leaders of the new day diverted energies to quantitative production. The capacity to do work, which the new methods in industry had so enormously increased, gave utilitarian objects an importance they had not hitherto possessed. Did not God's Word say: "Increase and multiply"? If babies, why not goods: if goods, why not dollars? Success was the Protestant miracle that justified man's ways to God.

The next figure that dominated the American scene stood even more completely for these new forces. He was, according to the pale lights of his time, a thoroughly cultivated man, and in his maturity he was welcomed in London and Paris as the equal of scientists like Priestley and Erasmus Darwin, and of scholars like D'Alembert and D'Holbach. As a citizen, by choice, of Philadelphia, Benjamin Franklin adopted the plain manners and simple thrifty ways of the Quakers. He went into business as a publisher, and with a sort of sweet acuteness in the pursuit of money, he imparted the secrets of his success in the collection of timely saws for which he became famous. The line from Franklin through Samuel Smiles to the latest advertise-

[35]

ments for improving one's position and doubling one's income, in the paper that dates back to Franklin's ownership, is a pretty direct one. If one prefers Franklin's bourgeois qualities to those of his successors, it is only perhaps because his life was more fully rounded. If he was not without the usurious habits of the financier, he had also the dignity and freedom of the true scientist.

For Franklin was equally the money-maker, the scientist, the inventor, and the politician, and in science his fair boast was that he had not gained a penny by any of his discoveries. He experimented with electricity; he invented the lightning rod; he improved the draft of chimneys; in fact, on his last voyage home to America, shortly before his death, he was still improving the draft of chimneys. Finally he was a Deist: he had gotten rid of all the "gothick phantoms" that seemed so puerile and unworthy to the quick minds of the Eighteenth Century—which meant that he was completely absorbed in the dominant abstractions and myths of his own time, namely, matter, money, and political rights. He accepted the mechanical concept of time: time is money; the importance of space: space must be conquered; the desirability of money: money must be made; and he did not see that these, too, are phantoms, in preoccupation with which a man may lose most of the advantages of a civilized life. As a young man, Franklin even invented an elaborate system of moral-bookkeeping: utilitarianism can go no further.

Although Franklin's sagacity as a statesman can hardly be overrated, for he had both patience and principle, the political side of the American thought of his time is best summed up in the doctrines of a new immigrant, that excellent friend of humanity, Thomas Paine. Paine's name has served so many purposes in polemics that scarcely any one seems to take the trouble to read his books: and so more than one shallow judgment has found its way into our histories of literature, written by worthy men who were incapable of enjoying a sound English style, or of following, with any pleasure, an honest system of thought, clearly expressed. The Rights of Man is as simple as a geometrical theorem; it contains, I think, most of what is valid in political libertarianism. I know of no other thinker who saw more clearly through the moral humbug that surrounds a good many theories of government. Said Paine:

"Almost everything appertaining to the circumstances of a nation has been absorbed and confounded under the general and mysterious word government. Though it avoids taking to its account the errors it commits and the mischiefs it occasions, it fails not to arrogate to itself whatever has the appearance of prosperity. It robs industry of its honors by pedantically making itself the cause of its effects; and purloins from the general character of man the merits that appertain to him as a social being."

Passage after passage in The Rights of Man and The Age of Reason is written with the same pithiness. Paine came to America as an adult, and saw the advantages of a fresh start. He believed that if first principles could be enunciated, here, and here alone, was a genuine opportunity to apply them. He summed up the hope in reason and in human contrivance that swelled through the Eighteenth Century. Without love for any particular country, and without that living sense of history which makes one accept the community's past, as one accepts the totality of one's own life, with all its lapses and mistakes, he was the vocal immigrant, justifying in his political and religious philosophy the complete break he had made with old ties, affections, allegiances.

Unfortunately, a man without a background is not more truly a man: he has merely lost the scenes and institutions which gave him his proper shape.

If one studies him closely, one will find that he has secretly arranged another background, made up of shadows that linger in the memory, or he is uneasy and restless, settles down, moves on, comes home again, lives on hopeless to-morrows, or sinks back into mournful yesterdays. The immigrants who came to America after the War of Independence gave up their fatherland in exchange for a Constitution and a Bill of Rights: they forfeited all the habits and institutions which had made them men without getting anything in exchange except freedom from arbitrary misrule. That they made the exchange willingly, proves that the conditions behind them were intolerable; but that the balance was entirely in favor of the new country, is something that we may well doubt. When the new settlers migrated in bodies, like the Moravians, they sometimes managed to maintain an affective cultural life; when they came alone, as "free individuals," they gained little more than cheap land and the privileges of the ballot box. The land itself was all to the good; and no one minded the change, or felt any lack, so long as he did not stop to compare the platitudes of Fourth of July orations with the actualities of the Slave Trade, the Constitutional Conventions, Alien and Sedition Acts, and Fugitive Slave Laws.

It was possible for Paine, in the Eighteenth Century, to believe that culture was served merely by the absence of a church, a state, a social order such as those under which Europe labored. That was the error of his school, for the absence of these harmful or obsolete institutions left a vacancy in society, and that vacancy was filled by work, or more accurately speaking, by busy work, which fatigued the body and diverted the mind from the things which should have enriched it. Republican politics aided this externalism. People sought to live by politics alone; the National State became their religion. The flag, as Professor Carleton Hayes has shown, supplanted the cross, and the Fathers of the Constitution the Fathers of the Church.

The interaction of the dominant interests of industry and politics is illustrated in Paine's life as well as Franklin's. Paine was the inventor of the take-down iron bridge. Indeed, politics and invention recurred rhythmically in his life, and he turned aside from his experiments on the iron bridge to answer Edmund Burke's attack on the French Revolution. "The War of Independence," as he himself said, "energized invention and lessened the catalogue of impossibilities. . . . As one among thousands who had borne a share in that memorable revolution, I returned with them to the enjoyment of a quiet life, and, that I might not be idle, undertook to construct a bridge of a single arch for this river [the Schuylkill]."

That I might not be idle! What a tale those words tell! While the aristocracy was in the ascendant, patient hirelings used to apply their knowledge of hydraulics to the working of fountains, as in Versailles, or they devised automatic chess-players, or they contrived elaborate clocks which struck the hour, jetted water, caused little birds to sing and wag their tails, and played selections from the operas. It was to such inane and harmless performances that the new skills in the exact arts were first put. The bored patron was amused; life plodded on; nothing was altered. But in the freedom of the new day, the common man, as indifferent to the symbols of the older culture as the great lords and ladies, innocent of anything to occupy his mind, except the notion of controlling matter and mastering the external world—the common man turned to inventions. Stupid folk drank heavily, ate gluttonously, and became libertines; intelligent, industrious men like Franklin and Paine, turned their minds to increasing the comforts and conveniences of existence. Justification by faith: that was politics: the belief in a new heaven and a new earth to be established by regular elections and parliamentary debate. Justification by works: that was invention. No frivolities entered this new religion. The new devices all saved labor, decreased distances, and in one way or another multiplied riches.

With these inventors, the American, like his contemporary in Europe, began the utilitarian conquest of his environment. From this time on, men with an imaginative bias like Morse, the pupil of Benjamin West, men like Whitney, the school-teacher, like Fulton, the miniature painter, turned to invention or at least the commercial exploitation of inventions without a qualm of distrust: to abandon the imaginative arts seemed natural and inevitable, and they no longer faced the situation, as the painters of the Renaissance had done, with a divided mind. Not that America began or monopolized the developments of the Industrial Revolution: the great outbreak of technical patents began, in fact, in England about 1760, and the first inklings of the movement were already jotted down in Leonardo da Vinci's notebooks. The point is that in Europe heavy layers of the old culture kept large sections of the directing classes in the old ways. Scholars, literary men, historians, artists still felt no need of justifying themselves by exclusive devotion to practical activities. In America, however, the old culture had worn thin, and in the rougher parts of the country it did not exist. No one in America was unaffected by the progress of invention; each improvement was quickly cashed in. When Stendhal wrote L'Amour the American love of comfort had already become a by-word: he refers to it with contempt.

Given an old culture in ruins, and a new culture *in vacuo*, this externalizing of interest, this ruthless exploitation of the physical environment was, it would seem, inevitable. Protestanism, science, invention, political democracy, all of these institutions denied the old values; all of them, by denial or by precept or by actual absorption, furthered the new activities. Thus in America the new order of Europe came quickly into being. If the Nineteenth Century found us more raw and rude, it was not because we had settled in a new territory; it was rather because our minds were not buoyed up by all those memorials of a great past that floated over the surface of Europe. The American was thus a stripped European; and the colonization of America can, with justice, be called the dispersion of Europe —a movement carried on by people incapable of sharing or continuing its past. It was to America that the outcast Europeans turned, without a Moses to guide them, to wander in the wilderness; and here they have remained in exile, not without an occasional glimpse, perhaps, of the promised land.

CHAPTER TWO

THE ROMANTICISM OF THE PIONEER

1

THE pioneer has usually been looked upon as a typical product of the American environment; but the truth is that he existed in the European mind before he made his appearance here. Pioneering may in part be described as the Romantic movement in action. If one wishes to fathom the pioneer's peculiar behavior, one must not merely study his relations with the Indians, with the trading companies, and with the government's land policies: one must also understand the main currents of European thought in the Eighteenth Century. In the episode of pioneering, a new system of ideas wedded itself to a new set of experiences: the experiences were American, but the ideas themselves had been nurtured in Savoy, in the English lake country, and on the Scots moors. Passing into action, these ideas became queerly transmogrified, so that it now takes more than a little digging to see the relation between Chateaubriand and Mark Twain, or Rousseau and William James. The pioneer arose out of an ex-

ternal opportunity, an unopened continent, and out
of an inward necessity. It is the inward necessity
that most of our commentators upon him have
neglected.

In the Eighteenth Century, Europe became at last
conscious of the fact that the living sources of its
older culture had dried up; and it made its first
attempt to find a basis for a new culture. Many of
its old institutions were already hollow and rotten.
The guilds had become nests of obsolete privileges,
which stood doggedly in the way of any technical improvement. The church, in England and in France,
had become an institution for providing support to
the higher ranks of the clergy, who believed only in
the mundane qualities of bread and wine. In fact,
all the remains of medieval Europe were in a state
of pitiable decay; they were like venerable apple-
trees, burgeoned with suckers and incapable of bearing fruit. A mere wind would have been enough to
send the old structure toppling; instead of it, a
veritable tempest arose, and by the time Voltaire had
finished with the Church, Montesquieu and Rousseau
with the State, Turgot and Adam Smith with the old
corporations, there was scarcely anything left that
an intelligent man of the Eighteenth Century would

have cared to carry away. Once the old shelters and
landmarks were gone, where could people turn?
The classic past had already been tried, and had
been found—dull. Medievalism was not yet quite
dead enough to be revived; *chinoiseries* were merely
amusing. There remained one great and permanent
source of culture, and with a hundred different gestures the Eighteenth Century acclaimed it—Nature.

The return to Nature occurred at the very climax
of an arranged and artificial existence: trees had
been clipped, hedges had been deformed, architecture
had become as cold and finicking as a pastrycook's
icing, the very hair of the human head had been
exchanged for the white wig of senility. Precisely at
this moment, when a purely urbane convention
seemed established forever, a grand retreat began.
In the Middle Ages such a retreat would have led
to the monastery: it now pushed back to the country, by valiant mountain paths, like Rousseau's, or
by mincing little country lanes, like that which led
Marie Antoinette to build an English village in Versailles, and play at being a milkmaid. Nature was
the fashion: "every one did it." If one had resources, one laid out a landscape park, wild like the
fells of Yorkshire, picturesque like the hills of Cum-

berland, the whole atmosphere heightened by an artificial ruin, to show dramatically the dominance of Nature over man's puny handiwork. If one were middle class, one built a villa, called Idle Hour, or The Hermitage; at the very least, one took country walks, or dreamed of a superb adventurous manhood in America.

In the mind of the great leader of this movement, Jean-Jacques Rousseau, Nature was not a fresh element in the tissue of European culture: it was a complete substitute for the existing institutions, conventions, habits, and histories. Rousseau began his career with an essay on the question whether the restoration of the arts and sciences had the effect of purifying or corrupting public morals: he won the prize offered by the academy at Dijon by affirming their tendency to corrupt; and from that time onward (1750) he continued to write, with better sense but with hardly any decrease in his turbulent conviction, upon the worthlessness of contemporary civilization in Europe. His prescription was simple: return to Nature: shun society: enjoy solitude. Rousseau's Nature was not Newton's Nature—a system of matter and motion, ordered by Providence, and established in the human mind by nice mathematical calculations. By Nature Rousseau meant the mountains, like those which shoulder across the background of his birthplace; he meant the mantle of vegetation, where one might botanize, and see "eternity in a grain of sand, and heaven in a wild flower;" he meant the fields, like those of Savoy, where a simple peasantry practiced the elementary routine of living.

The return to Nature, in Rousseau's sense, was not a new injunction; nor was it an unsound one. As an aid to recovery in physical illness and neurosis, its value was recognized at least as early as Hippocrates, and as a general social formula it has played a part in the life and literature of every finished civilization. The Georgics, the Bucolics, and the idylls of classic culture belong to its sophisticated moments: after the formalities of the Confucian period Lao-tse's philosophy developed a similar creed and persuaded its individualistic adherents to renounce the sterile practices of the court and the bureaucracy and bury themselves in the Bamboo Grove. Nature almost inevitably becomes dominant in the mind when the powers of man himself to mold his fortunes and make over his institutions seem feeble—when, in order to exist at all, it is necessary to accept the wilderness of Nature and human passion as "given," without trying to subdue its disorder.

What made the authority of Rousseau's doctrine so immense, what made it play such a presiding part in European life, echoing through the minds of Goethe, Herder, Kant, Wordsworth, and even, quite innocently, Blake, was the fact that there awaited the European in America a Nature that was primitive and undefiled. In the purely mythical continent that uprose in the European mind, the landscape was untainted by human blood and tears, and the Red Indian, like Atala, led a life of physical dignity and spiritual austerity: the great Sachem was an aborigine with the stoic virtues of a Marcus Aurelius. Rousseau's glorification of peasant life was after all subject to scrutiny, and by the time the French Revolution came, the peasant had a word or two to say about it himself; but the true child of Nature in the New World, uncorrupted by the superstitions of the Church, could be idealized to the heart's content: his customs could be attributed to the unhindered spontaneity of human nature, his painfully acquired and transmitted knowledge might be laid to instinctive processes; in short, he became a pure ideal. Even William Blake could dream of

liberty on the banks of the Ohio, if not on the banks
of the Thames.

In America, if society was futile, one had only
to walk half a day to escape it; in Europe, if one
walked half a day one would be in the midst of
another society. In Europe one had to *plan* a retreat: in America one simply encountered it. If
Nature was, as Wordsworth said, a world of ready
wealth, blessing our minds and hearts with wisdom
and health and cheerfulness, what place could be
richer than America? Once Romanticism turned its
eyes across the ocean, it became a movement indeed.
It abandoned culture to return to Nature; it left a
skeleton of the past for an embryo of the future; it
renounced its hoarded capital and began to live on
its current income; it forfeited the old and the tried
for the new and the experimental. This transformation was, as Nietzsche said, an immense physiologi-
cal process, and its result was "the slow emergence of
an essentially super-national and nomadic species of
man, who possesses, physiologically speaking, a maxi-
mum of the art and power of adaptation as his typical distinction."

The Romantic Movement was thus the great formative influence which produced not merely the myth
of pioneering, but the pioneer. But it was not the

sole influence upon the scene. Human society was divided in the Eighteenth Century between those who thought it perfectible, and those who thought that the existing institutions were all essentially rotten: the Benthams and the Turgots were on one side, the Rousseaus and Blakes on the other, and the great mass of people mixed these two incompatible doctrines in varying proportions. The perfectionists believed in progress, science, laws, education, and comfort; progress was the mode and comfort the end of every civil arrangement. The followers of Rousseau believed in none of these things. Instead of sense, they wanted sensibility; instead of education, spontaneity; instead of smokeless chimneys and glass windows and powerlooms, a clear sky and an open field.

If the pioneer was the lawfully begotten child of the Romantic Movement, he belonged to the other school by adoption. He wanted Nature; and he wanted comfort no less. He sought to escape the conventions of society; yet his notion of a free government was one that devoted itself to a perpetual process of legislation, and he made no bones about appealing to the Central Government when he wanted inland waterways and roads and help in exterminating the Indian. Society was effete: its machinery could be perfected—the pioneer accepted both these notions. He believed with Rousseau that "man is good naturally, and that by institutions only is he made bad." And if the Yankees who first settled in Illinois were looked upon as full of "notions" because they were wont to take thought for the morrow and to multiply mechanical devices, these habits, too, were quickly absorbed. As Nature grew empty, progress took its place in the mind of the pioneer. Each of these ideas turned him from the past, and enabled him to speculate, in both the commercial and philosophic senses of the word, on the future.

II

In America the return to Nature set in before there was any physical necessity for filling up the raw lands of the West. The movement across the Alleghanies began long before the East was fully occupied: it surged up in the third quarter of the Eighteenth Century, after the preliminary scouting and road-building by the Ohio Company, and by the time the Nineteenth Century was under way, the conquest of the Continent had become the obsession of every progressive American community.

This westward expansion of the pioneer was, without doubt, furthered by immediate causes, such as the migration of disbanded soldiers after the Revolution, endowed with land-warrants; but from the beginning, the movement was compulsive and almost neurotic; and as early as 1837 Peck's New Guide to the West recorded that "migration has become almost a habit." External matters of fact would perhaps account for the New England migration to Ohio: they cease to be relevant, however, when they are called upon to explain the succession of jumps which caused so many settlers to pull up stakes and move into Illinois—and then into Missouri—and so beyond, until finally the Pacific Coast brought the movement temporarily to an end. This restless search was something more than a prospecting of resources; it was an experimental investigation of Nature, Solitude, The Primitive Life; and at no stage of the journey, however much the story may be obscured by land-booms and Indian massacres and gold rushes, did these things drop out of the pioneer's mind. Charles Fenno Hoffmann in A Winter in the West (1835), was only echoing the unconscious justification of the pioneer when he exclaimed: "What is the echo of roofs that a few centuries since rung with barbaric revels, or of aisles that pealed the anthems of painted pomp, to the silence which has reigned in these dim groves since the first fiat of Creation was spoken?"

Mark the difference between this movement and that which first planted the colonists of Massachusetts or Pennsylvania in the New World. In the first period of the seaboard settlement, America was a place where the European could remain more nearly his proper self, and keep up the religious practices which were threatened by economic innovations and political infringements in Europe. The Puritans, the Moravians, the Dunkers, the Quakers, the Catholics, sought America as a refuge in which they could preserve in greater security what they dearly valued in Europe. But with the drift to the West, America became, on the contrary, a place where the European could be swiftly transformed into something different: where the civil man could become a hardy savage, where the social man could become an "individual," where the settled man could become a nomad, and the family man could forget his old connections. With pioneering, America ceased to be an outpost of Europe. The Western communities relapsed into an earlier and more primitive type of occupation; they reverted to the crude practices of the hunter, the woodman, and the miner. Given the occasion and the environment, these were necessary occupations; the point to be noted, however, is that, uninfluenced by peasant habits or the ideas of an old culture, the work of the miner, woodman, and hunter led to unmitigated destruction and pillage. What happened was just the reverse of the old barbarian invasions, which turned the Goths and the Vandals into Romans. The movement into backwoods America turned the European into a barbarian.

The grisly process of this settlement was described by Crèvecœur and Cooper long before Professor Turner summed them up in his classic treatise on the passing of the frontier. "In all societies," says Crèvecœur, "there are off-casts; this impure part serves as our precursors or pioneers. . . . By living in or near the woods, their actions are regulated by the neighborhood. The deer often come to eat their grain, the wolves to destroy their sheep, the bears to kill their hogs, the foxes to catch their poultry. The surrounding hostility immediately puts the gun into their hands; they watch these animals; they kill some; and thus, by defending their property, they soon become professed hunters; this is the progress; once hunters, farewell to the plow. The chase renders them ferocious, gloomy, unsociable; a hunter wants no neighbors, he rather hates them because he dreads competition."

Equipped with his ax and his rifle, the two principal weapons of the pioneer, he carried on his warfare against Nature, cutting down the forest and slaughtering its living creatures. Instead of seeking Nature in a wise passiveness, as Wordsworth urged, he raped his new mistress in a blind fury of obstreperous passion. No one who has read The Pioneers can forget Cooper's account of the sickening massacre of wild pigeons, carried on long after the need for food had been satisfied. In these practices, the ordinary farmer and tradesman of the old country went back to a phase of European experience which had lingered on chiefly in the archaic hunts of a predatory aristocracy; and in the absence of any restraints or diversions, these primitive practices sank more deeply into the grain.

The apology for this behavior was based upon the noblest grounds; one can scarcely pick up a contemporary description of the pioneering period without finding a flowery account of the new life, put in contrast to wretched, despotic, foolishly beautiful Europe; and this animus was echoed even in the comments that Hawthorne and Emerson, to say nothing of such a real pioneer as Mark Twain, made upon the institutions of the Old World. Let me put the contemporary apology and criticism side by side. The first is from a pamphlet by George Lunt called Three Eras of New England (1857):

"Whenever this is the state of man the impertinent fictions and sophisms of life die out. The borrowings and lendings of the human creature fall away from him under the rigid discipline of primeval necessities, as the encrusting dirt, which bedimmed the diamond, is removed by the hard process which reveals and confirms its inestimable price. The voice of the mountain winds would mock at the most indispensable and best recognized trappings of polished society as they rent them away and fastened them fluttering in the crevices of a cliff, or bore them onwards to the unknown wilderness, and would hail its very discomforts with the shout and laughter of derision. . . . So far, therefore, as our familiar and inherent characteristics, which form the foundation of our nature, and make us good and make us great, are liable to become diluted or perverted by the sophistications of social being, they may require an actual refreshment and renewal, under the severe and inevitable trials of colonial existence. . . . This, then, is the absolute law of all legitimate migration, that it leaves behind it the weaknesses, the concretions and

superfluities of artificial life, and founds its new
existence upon an appeal to the primordial elements
of natural society."

Against this apology for the deprivations of the
pioneer life, let me set the comment of a young English settler named Fordham, who had come face to
face with the untrammeled Children of Nature; this
passage occurs on the page after that in which he
records the amiable slaughter of six Indians, men
and women, on English Prairie, in the spring of
1817:

"Instead of being more virtuous, as he is less refined, I am inclined to think that man's virtues are
like the fruits of the earth, only excellent when subjected to culture. The force of the simile you will
never feel, until you ride in these woods over wild
strawberries, which dye your horses' fetlocks like
blood, yet are insipid in flavour; till you have seen
wagon-loads of grapes, choked by the brambles and
the poisonous vine; till you find peaches, tasteless
as a turnip, and roses throwing their leaves of every
shade upon the wind, with scarcely a scent upon
them. 'Tis the hand of man that makes the wilderness shine."

The hand of man was of course busy, and here
and there, particularly in Ohio, Kentucky and

Tennessee, villages and cities grew up which carried on, for a generation or so in the Nineteenth Century, the tradition that the seaboard knew in an earlier day; but like a river that, rushing onwards, deposits its heaviest burdens first, the best people and the soundest traditions tended to be deposited in the tracts that adjoined the original colonies, and as the stream moved further west, the traditions of a civil life disappeared, and the proportion of scalawags, cut-throats, bruisers, bullies, and gamblers tended to increase, and the wilderness got the upper hand. There are plenty of exceptions to this generalization, it goes without saying; but Texas and Nevada were the poles towards which pioneer effort tended to run. The original process has been obscured in many places by a second and third wave of agriculturists: but it is not hard to get below the surface and see what the original reality was.

III

The shock of the pioneer's experience left its mark in one or two gestures of anticipation, and in an aftermath of regretful reminiscence. The post-Civil War writers who deal with Roughing It, A Son of the Middle Border, or A Hoosier School-

master, to mention only a few examples, had already
abandoned the scene of the pioneer's efforts and had
returned to the East: they made copy of their early
life, but, though they might be inclined to sigh after
it, because it was associated with their youth, they
had only a sentimental notion of continuing it. For
them, the pioneering experience could be recapitu-
lated in a night around a camp-fire or a visit to the
Wild West Show, which the astute Barnum had introduced to the denizens of New York in a day when
the West was still in fact wild. A genuine culture and
a relevant way of life do not lose their significance
so easily; and the thin-skinnedness of the pioneer
in the face of criticism, and the eagerness of the
post-pioneer generation—The Inheritors of Susan
Glaspell's play—to identify themselves with the culture of the past, shows, I think, that at bottom the
pioneer realized that his efforts had gone awry.

One is faced by the paradox that the formative
elements in the pioneer's career expressed themselves in literature almost at the very outset of the
movement, in the works of men who were in fact almost as aloof from the realities of the western exodus
as Chateaubriand himself; and although the pioneer
types and the pioneer adventures have been repeated
in literature of the rubber-stamp pattern from

Gustav Aimard to Zane Gray, what was valid and what was peculiar in the pioneer regime was embodied, once for all, by James Fenimore Cooper. These new contacts, these new scenes, these adventures, served to create just three genuine folk-heroes. In these heroes, the habits of the pioneer were raised to the plane of a pattern.

Cooper's Leatherstocking was the new *Natur-Mensch,* established on a platform of simple human dignity. He was versed in the art of the woods, with the training of the aborigine himself; he shared the reticence and shyness that the Amerind perhaps showed in the company of strangers; and above the tender heart he exhibited mutely in The Deerslayer, he disclosed a leathery imperturbability. His eye was unerring; and it was only in instinct that Chingachgook, the Indian, sometimes surpassed this great hunter and warrior. Leatherstocking's bullet, which drives the bullet that has already hit the bull's eye still deeper into the target is, of course, no ordinary bullet: it shared the inevitable enlargement of the hero's powers. Not every pioneer, needless to say, was a Natty Bumpo; but the shy, reserved, taciturn, dryly humorous hunter was the sort of being the pioneer tended, under the first stress of his new association, to become. Cooper himself painted other pioneer types, the sullen squatter, Ishmael, the fur trader, the frontier soldier, the woodman, the bee-hunter; but the fact that he had already outlined the character of Leatherstocking in the equally shrewd and reserved Spy of the Neutral Ground, Harvey Birch, showed, I believe, that this figure had become a property of his unconscious.

First a hunter, then a scout, then a trapper, Leatherstocking encompassed the chief pioneering experiences; it required a generation or two before the trader became the boomtown manufacturer, and the manufacturer the realtor and financier, dealing only with the tokens of industry. Like the first pioneers, Leatherstocking fled before the smoke of the settler's domestic fire, as before the prairie fire itself. With all the shoddiness of Cooper's imaginative constructions, he was plainly seized by a great character: his novels live solely through their central conception of Leatherstocking. The hard man, a Sir Giles Overreach, or the cunning man, Ulysses, had been portrayed before in literature; but the hardness and craft of Leatherstocking brought forth a new quality, which came directly from the woods and the prairies. When the pioneer called his first political hero Old Hickory he poetically expressed this new truth of character: barbarians or outlaws they might be, these pioneers, but their heroes grew straight. This straightness is the great quality one feels in Lincoln. It was as if, after centuries of clipping and pruning, we had at last allowed a tree to grow to its full height, shaped only by snow, rain, sun, wind, frost. A too timid and complacent culture may sacrifice the inner strength to an agreeable conformity to a common mold, a little undersized. These Old Hickories, on the other hand, grew a little scraggly and awkward; but in their reach, one would catch, occasionally, a hint of the innate possibilities of the species.

In the course of the Nineteenth Century, Leatherstocking was joined by an even more authentic folk hero, Paul Bunyan, whose gigantic shape, partly perhaps derived from Gargantua through his French-Canadian forebears, took form over the fire in the logger's shack. Paul Bunyan, properly enough, was an axman; and, as if to complete the symbolism and identify himself more completely with the prime activities of the new American type, he was also a great inventor. He figures on a continental scale. All his prowess and strength is based upon the notion that a thing becomes a hundred times as important if it is a hundred times as big. The habit of counting and "calculating" and "figuring" and "reckoning" and "guessing"—the habit, that is, of exchanging quality for number—is expressed in nearly all of Bunyan's exploits. In a day when no one dared point to the string of shacks that formed the frontier town as a proof of the qualitative beauties and delights of a pioneer community, the popular imagination took refuge in a statistical criterion of value: they counted heads: they counted money: they counted miles: they counted anything that lent itself to large figures.

This habit grew to such an extent that people began to appreciate its comic quality; in the Bunyan tales it is a device of humor as well as of heroic exaggeration. For many years, as the legend was quietly growing and expanding, Paul Bunyan lurked under the surface of our life: we lived by his light, even if we were ignorant of his legend. He, too, like Leatherstocking, was aloof from women; and this fact is not without significance; for with the woman the rough bachelor life must come to an end, and though the pioneer might carry his family with him, bedstead, baby, and all, they were sooner or later bound to domesticate him, and make him settle down. Woman was the chief enemy of the pioneer: she courageously rose to the burdens of the new life, and demanded her place side by side in the legislature: but in the end she had her revenge, in temperance clubs, in anti-vice societies, or in the general tarnation tidiness of Tom Sawyer's aunt. When Whitman sang of the Perfect Comrade, he did not at first think of woman: so far from indicating a special sexual anomaly in Whitman, it is rather a tribute to his imaginative identification with the collective experience of his generation.

At the same time, another folk-hero arose in literature, at first sight an incomprehensible one. He was neither heroic, nor, on the surface, a pioneer; and the story that brought him forth was a rather commonplace fantasy of an earlier day. Yet the history of Rip Van Winkle shows that he has had a deep hold on the American mind: Irving's tale itself remains a popular legend, and the play that was written about him as early as the eighteen-thirties was remodeled by succeeding generations of American actors, until given its classic form by Joseph Jefferson. How did this happen? The reason, I think, was that Rip's adventures and disappointments stood for that of the typical American of the pioneer period. Inept at consecutive work, harried by his wife, and disgusted with human society, he retires to the hills with his dog and his gun. He drinks heavily, falls asleep, and becomes

enchanted. At the end of twenty years he awakes
to find himself in a different society. The old landmarks have gone; the old faces have disappeared;
all the outward aspects of life have changed. At
the bottom, however, Rip himself has not changed;
for he has been drunk and lost in a dream, and for all
that the calendar and the clock records, he remains,
mentally, a boy.

There was the fate of a whole generation: indeed, is it not still the fate of perhaps the great
majority of Americans, lost in their dreams of a
great fortune in real-estate, rubber, or oil? In our
heroic moments, we may think of ourselves as
Leatherstockings, or two-fisted fellows like Paul
Bunyan; but in the bottom of our hearts, we are
disconsolate Rips. In this process of uneasy transition, in the endless experimentalism and externality
of the American scheme, the American came to feel
that something was wrong. He saw no way of
rectifying the fact itself; the necessity to be "up
and moving" seemed written in the skies. In his disappointment and frustration, he became maudlin.
It is no accident that our most sentimental popular
songs all date back to the earlier half of the Nineteenth Century. At the moment when the eagle
screamed loudest, when the words Manifest Destiny

were put into circulation, when Colonel Diver, the fire-eater, Jefferson Brick, the editor of the Rowdy Journal, and Scadder, the real-estate gambler, were joining voices in a Hallelujah of triumph,—it was then that the tear of regret and the melancholy clutch of the Adam's apple made their way into the ballad.

The great song of the mid-century was "Don't you remember Sweet Alice, Ben Bolt?" but the truth is that Alice was merely a name to start the tears rolling. It was not over the fate of Alice that the manly heart grieved: what hurt was the fact that in the short space of twenty years, the mill-wheel had fallen to pieces, the rafters had tumbled in, the cabin had gone to ruin, the tree had been felled, and "where once the lord of the forest waved" were grass and golden grain. In short, ruin and change lay in the wake of the pioneer, as he went westering. "There is change in the things I loved, Ben Bolt, they have changed from the old to the new," and somehow this progressive generation had an uneasy suspicion that they were not changing altogether for the better. What a conflict was in the pioneer's bosom! He pulls up stakes, to the tune of Home Sweet Home. He sells his parcel of real estate to the next gambler who will hold it, still sighing "there is no place like home." He guts out the forest: "Woodman, spare that tree, touch not a single bough, in youth it sheltered me, and I'll protect it now." And in the struggle of scalping one of the Red Varmints he is driving to the Land of the Sunset the Song of Hiawatha slips from his hip-pocket.

Does this seem to exaggerate the conflict? Be assured that it was there. The Mark Twains, Bret Hartes, and Artemus Wards would not have found the old solidities of Europe so ingratiating, taught as they were to despise Europe's cities and institutions as the relics of a miserable and feudal past, if the life they had known had not too often starved their essential humanity.

IV

With the experience of the Great War behind us, we can now understand a little better the psychal state of our various American communities, whilst they were immersed in their besetting "war against Nature." A war automatically either draws people into the service, or, if they resist, unfits them for carrying on their civil duties in a whole-hearted manner. In the pioneer's war against Nature, every member of the community was bound to take

part, or be branded as a dilettante, a skulker, a
deserter.   The phrases that were used in justification of pioneering during the Nineteenth Century
were not those which set the Romantic Movement in
action in the Eighteenth: these newcomers sought to
"conquer a wilderness," "subdue Nature," "take
possession of the continent."   "To act that each
to-morrow finds us *farther* than to-day," was the
very breath of the new pioneer mores: the Psalm of
Life was the sum of the pioneer's life.

The throb and urge of this grand march across
the continent communicated itself to those who remained in the East.   The non-combatants in Boston,
Philadelphia, and New York were as uneasy and
hesitating in their activities as a conscript who expects at any moment to be called to the colors.
Some of them, like C. F. Adams, were only too happy
when the Civil War turned the call of the pioneer
into a command; others, like William Perkins Marsh
confessed that "in our place and day the scholar
hath no vocation," and made plain with what reluctance they turned their backs upon science and the
humane arts to struggle in the world of business;
others, like William Cullen Bryant, threw a handful
of Nature poems into the scales, to weigh over
against a life of zealous energy in newspaperdom.

The Romanticism of the Pioneer

In these, and many other equally irritating biographies, one finds that the myth of the Pioneer Conquest had taken possession of even the finer and more sensitive minds: they accepted the uglinesses and brutalities of pioneering, even as many of our contemporaries accepted the bestialities of war, and instead of recognizing no other necessity than their best desires, they throttled their desires and bowed to an imaginary necessity. In the end, the pioneer was as far from Rousseau and Wordsworth as the inventor of poison gas was from the troubadour who sang the Song of Roland.

The effect of the pioneer habits upon our culture has become a commonplace of literary criticism during the last half-generation; the weakness of this criticism has been the failure to grasp the difference in origin between the puritan, the pioneer, and the inventor-business man. The Puritan did indeed pave the way for the extroverts that came after him; but what he really sought was an inner grace. The pioneer debased all the old values of a settled culture, and made the path of a dehumanized industrialism in America as smooth as a concrete road; but it was only in the habits he had developed, so to say, on the road, that he turned aside from the proper goal of the Romantic Movement, which was to find a basis for a fresh effort in culture, and gave himself over to the inventor-businessman's search for power. All three, Puritan, pioneer, and businessman came to exist through the breakdown of Europe's earlier, integrated culture; but, given the wide elbow room of America, each type tended to develop to its extreme, only to emerge in succeeding generations into the composite character of that fictitious person, the Average American.

In order to appreciate the distance between the America of the Eighteenth Century, which was still attached umbilically to the older Europe, and the America of the pioneer, tinctured by the puritan and the industrialist, one might perhaps compare two representative men, Thomas Jefferson and Mark Twain. When Mark Twain went to Europe during the Gilded Age, he was really an innocent abroad: his experience in Roughing It had not fitted him for any sort of seasoned contact with climates, councils, governments. When Jefferson went to Paris from the backwoods of Virginia, a hundred years earlier, he was a cultivated man, walking among his peers: he criticized English architecture, not as Mark Twain might have done, because it was effete and feudal, but because it was even more barbarous than that of the American provinces. To Mark Twain,

as to most of his contemporaries, industry appeared
in the light of what sporting people call a good
thing; when, after sinking a small fortune in a new
typesetting machine, he approached his friend H. H.
Rogers with another invention, the chief attraction
he emphasized was its potential monopoly. Jefferson's concern with the practical arts, on the other
hand, was personal and esthetic: he was an active
farmer, with a carefully kept nursery book, and he
brought back to America prints and measurements
of public buildings, which served him in the design
of his own.

The death of Jefferson, the scholar, the artist,
the statesman, and agriculturist—one of the last
true figures of the Renaissance—was symbolic; for
it came in 1826, just at the moment when the great
westward expansion began. In two men of the following generation, S. F. B. Morse and Edgar Allen
Poe, we find the new pioneer mores working towards
their two legitimate goals. Morse defended his preoccupation with criticism, instead of painting, in
words that might have been framed as an illustration
of the mood I have been trying to describe. "If I
am to be the Pioneer, and am fitted for it, why should
I not glory as much in felling trees and clearing away
rubbish as in showing the decorations suited to a

more advanced state of culture?" As for Poe, the
Walpole of a belated Gothic revival, he recorded in
literature the displacement and dissociation that
was taking place in the community's life.

With no conscious connection with the life about
him, Poe became nevertheless the literary equivalent
of the industrialist and the pioneer. I have no desire
to speak lightly of Poe's capacities as a critic of
literature, which were high, nor of his skill in the
formal exercises of literary composition. Poe was
the first artist consciously to give the short-story
a succinct and final form; and as an esthetic ex-
perimentalist his own arrangements in prose prepared the way, among other things, for Baudelaire's
prose poems. Yet Poe's meticulous and rationalistic
mind fitted his environment and mirrored its inner
characteristics far more readily than a superficial
look at it would lead one to believe. In him, the
springs of human desire had not so much frozen up
as turned to metal: his world was, in one of his
favorite words, plutonian, like that of Watt and
Fulton and Gradgrind: the tears that he dropped
were steel beads, and his mind worked like a mechanical hopper, even when there were no appropriate
materials to throw into it. It happened to be a
very good mind; and when it had something valu-

able to work upon, as in literary criticism, the results were often excellent. Left to himself, however, he either spent his energies on small ingenuities like ciphers and "scientific" puzzles, or he created a synthetic world, half-pasteboard and half-perfume, whose thinness as an imaginative reality was equaled only by its apparent dissociation from the actualities that surrounded him. The criticism of Poe's fantasies is not that they were "unreal": Shakespeare's are equally so: the criticism is that they have their sources in a starved and limited humanity, the same starved and limited humanity in which Gradgrind devoted himself to "hard facts," and the frontier fighter to cold steel. Terror and cruelty dominated Poe's mind; and terror and cruelty leave a scar on almost every tale and anecdote about pioneer life.

The emotional equivalence of Poe's fiction and the pioneer's fact was perhaps a matter of chance; I will not strain my point by trying to make out a case for anything else. That the equivalence is not a meretricious presumption on my part, is attested, I think, by the fact that it was corroborated a generation later in the anecdotes of Mark Twain and the short stories of Ambrose Bierce. No sensitive mind can undergo warfare or pioneering, with all the raw savagery of human nature developed to the full, without undergoing a shock. The massacres, the banditries, even the coarse practical jokes, all left their detestable impressions. There is a mock-sinister side to the Romantic Movement in European literature in the horror stories of Walpole and Mrs. Radcliffe; but these stories are mere pap for infants alongside those Mark Twain was able to recount in almost every chapter of Roughing It and Life on the Mississippi.

Poe, perhaps, had never heard one of these stories; but the dehumanized world he created gave a place for terrors, cruelties, and murders which expressed, in a sublimated and eminently readable form, the sadisms and masochisms of the pioneer's life. Man is, after all, a domestic animal; and though he may return to unbroken nature as a relief from all the sobrieties of existence, he can reside for long in the wilderness only by losing some of the essential qualities of the cultivated human species. Poe had lost these qualities, neurotically, without even seeing the wilderness. Cooper's generation had dreamed of Leatherstocking; in realization, the dream had become the nightmare world of Poe. There is scarcely a page of reliable testimony about pioneer life which does not hint at this nightmare. The testimony is all the more salient when one finds

Mark Twain reciting his horrors in a vein of pure innocence, without a word of criticism, and then, by a psychic transfer, becoming ferociously indignant over the same things when he finds them in his imaginary Court of King Arthur.

v

The vast gap between the hope of the Romantic Movement and the reality of the pioneer period is one of the most sardonic jests of history. On one side, the bucolic innocence of the Eighteenth Century, its belief in a fresh start, and its attempt to achieve a new culture. And over against it, the epic march of the covered wagon, leaving behind it deserted villages, bleak cities, depleted soils, and the sick and exhausted souls that engraved their epitaphs in Mr. Masters' Spoon River Anthology. Against the genuine heroism and derring-do that accompanied this movement, and against the real gains that it achieved here and there in the spread of social well-being, must be set off the crudities of the pioneer's sexual life, his bestial swilling and drinking and bullying, and his barbarities in dealing with the original inhabitants—"a fierce dull biped standing in our way." The gun and the ax and the pick, alas! had taught their lessons only too well; and the more social and coöperative groups, like the Mormons, were attacked violently, but always under the cover of high moral indignation, by belligerent worthies whose morals would have given a bad odor to a hangman's picnic.

The truth is that the life of the pioneer was bare and insufficient: he did not really face Nature, he merely evaded society. Divorced from its social context, his experience became meaningless. That is why, perhaps, he kept on changing his occupation and his habitat, for as long as he could keep on moving he could forget that, in his own phrase, he was not "getting anywhere." He had no end of experiences: he could shoot, build, plant, chop, saw, dicker: he was Ulysses, Nimrod, Noah, and Cain all bundled into one man. But there was, all too literally, no end to these activities—that is, no opportunity to refine them, to separate the ore from the slag, to live them over again in the mind. In short, the pioneer experience did not produce a rounded pioneer culture; and if the new settler began as an unconscious follower of Rousseau, he was only too ready, after the first flush of effort, to barter all his glorious heritage for gas light and paved streets and starched collars and skyscrapers and the other insignia of a truly high and progressive civilization. The return to Nature led, ironically, to a denatured environment, and when, after the long journey was over, the pioneer became conscious once more of the social obligation, these interests manifested themselves in covert pathological ways, like campaigns to prohibit the cigarette or to prescribe the length of sheets for hotel beds, or to promote institutions of compulsory good fellowship. So much for an experience that failed either to absorb an old culture or create a new one!

CHAPTER THREE

THE GOLDEN DAY

THE MORNING STAR

No one who was awake in the early part of the
Nineteenth Century was unaware that in the practical arrangements of life men were on the brink of
a great change. The rumble of the industrial revolution was heard in the distance long before the
storm actually broke; and before American society
was completely transformed through the work of
the land-pioneer and the industrial pioneer, there
arose here and there over the land groups of people
who anticipated the effects of this revolution and
were in revolt against all its preoccupations. Some
of these groups reverted to an archaic theocracy,
like that of the Mormons, in which a grotesque body
of beliefs was combined with an extraordinary
amount of economic sagacity and statesmanship;
some of them became disciples of Fourier and sought
to live in coöperative colonies, which would foster
men's various capacities more fully than the utilitarian community.

The Golden Day

The air quivered with both hope and trepidation. In the new industrial cities, the slum made its appearance; great bodies of depauperate immigrants with strange traditions altered the balance of power; politics became the business of clever rapscallions who looted the public treasury; by the end of the fifties an editorial writer in Harper's Weekly prayed for professional administrators who might bring a public consience into the corrupt democracy of the big cities. In general, all the forces that blighted America after the Civil War existed in embryonic form between 1830 and 1860. At the same time, the older regions began to reap the fruits of two centuries of contact with the new soil and new customs. It is at the hour when the old ways are breaking up that men step outside them sufficiently to feel their beauty and significance: lovers are often closest at the moment of parting. In New England, the inherited medieval civilization had become a shell; but, drying up, it left behind a sweet acrid aroma, and for a brief day it had a more intense existence in the spirit. Before the life itself collapsed, men felt the full weight of it in their imagination. In the act of passing away, the Puritan begot the Transcendentalist, and the will-to-power, which had made him what he was, with his firm but forbidding character, and his conscientious but narrow activity, gave way to the will-to-perfection.

The period from 1830 to 1860 was in America one of disintegration and fulfillment: the new and the old, the crude and the complete, the base and the noble mingled together. Puritan fanatics like Goodyear brought to the vulcanization of rubber the same intense passion that Thoreau brought to Nature: sharp mountebanks like Barnum grew out of the same sort of Connecticut village that nourished an inspired schoolmaster like Bronson Alcott: genuine statesmen like Brigham Young organized the colonization of Utah whilst nonentities like Pierce and Buchanan governed the whole country. During this period, the old culture of the seaboard settlement had its Golden Day in the mind; the America of the migrations, on the other hand, partly because of weaknesses developed in the pioneer, partly because of the one-sided interests of the industrialist, and partly because of the volcanic eruption of the Civil War had up to 1890 little more than the boomtown optimism of the Gilded Age to justify its existence.

The Golden Day

Despite the foreboding that every intelligent mind felt when it contemplated the barbarism of the industrial age, inimical to any culture except that which grew out of its own inhuman absorption in abstract matter and abstract power, the dominant note of the period was one of hope. Before the Civil War the promise of the Westward march expanded the sense of achievement that came over the Eastern States; and men faced the world with a confidence that went beyond the complacent optimism of the British Utilitarians—tainted as that was by Carlyle's dire reminders of the palpable wreckage and jetsam that had been washed into the slums of London, Manchester, and Birmingham on the wave of "industrial prosperity."

There were no Carlyles or Ruskins in America during this period; they were almost unthinkable. One might live in this atmosphere, or one might grapple with the White Whale and die; but if one lived, one lived without distrust, without inner complaint, and even if one scorned the ways of one's fellows, as Thoreau did, one remained among them, and sought to remedy in oneself the abuses that existed in society. Transcendentalism might criticize a fossilized past; but no one imagined that the

future could be equally fossilized. The testimony
is unqualified. One breathed hope, as one might
breathe the heady air of early autumn, pungent
with the smell of hickory fires and baking bread, as
one walked through the village street.

"One cannot look on the freedom of this country,
in connection with its youth," wrote Emerson in
The Young American, "without a presentment that
here shall laws and institutions exist in some proportion to the majesty of Nature. . . . It is a country
of beginnings, of projects, of vast designs and expectations. It has no past: all has an onward and pro-
spective look." The voice of Whitman echoed Emerson through a trumpet: but that of Melville, writing in 1850, was no less sanguine and full-pulsed:
"God has predestinated, mankind expects, great
things from our race; and great things we feel
in our souls. The rest of the nations must soon
be in our rear. We are the pioneers of the world;
the advance guard, sent on through the wilderness
of untried things, to break a new path in the New
World that is ours. In our youth is our strength;
in our inexperience, our wisdom."

"Every institution is the lengthened shadow of a
man." Here and there in America during its Golden

Day grew up a man who cast a shadow over the landscape. They left no labor-saving machines, no discoveries, and no wealthy bequests to found a library or a hospital: what they left was something much less and much more than that—an heroic conception of life. They peopled the landscape with their own shapes. This period nourished men, as no other has done in America before or since. Up to that time, the American communities were provincial; when it was over, they had lost their base, and spreading all over the landscape, deluged with newcomers speaking strange languages and carrying on Old-World customs, they lost that essential likeness which is a necessary basis for intimate communication. The first settlement was complete: agricultural and industrial life were still in balance in the older parts of the country; and on the seas trade opened up activities for the adventurous. When Ticknor was preparing to go to Germany, in the first decade of the century, there was but one German dictionary, apparently, in New England. Within a generation, Goethe was translated, selections from the European classics were published; and importations of the Indian, Chinese and Persian classics widened the horizon of people who had known India only by its shawls, China only by its tea.

The Golden Day

The traffic of the American merchantman across the seas brought ideas with every load of goods. Living lustily in all these new experiences, the pushing back of the frontier, the intercourse with the Ancient East, the promises of science and invention—steamboats: railroads: telegraphs: rubber raincoats: reapers: Von Baer: Faraday: Darwin:— living in these things, and believing in them, the capacity for philosophic exploration increased, too; and when an Emerson went into retreat, he retired with an armful of experiences and ideas comparable only to the treasuries that the Elizabethans grandly looted. Within the circle of the daily fact, the Transcendentalists might protest against the dull materialism which was beginning to dominate the period: but it needed only a little boldness to convert the materialism itself into a source of new potencies.

An imaginative New World came to birth during this period, a new hemisphere in the geography of the mind. That world was the climax of American experience. What preceded led up to it: what followed, dwindled away from it; and we who think and write to-day are either continuing their first exploration, or we are disheartened, and relapse into some stale formula, or console ourselves with empty gestures of frivolity.

The American scene was a challenge; and men rose to it. The writers of this period were not alone; if they were outcasts in the company of the usual run of merchants, manufacturers, and politicians, they were at all events attended by a company of people who had shared their experience and moved on eagerly with it. When all is reckoned, however, there is nothing in the minor writers that is not pretty fully recorded by Emerson, Thoreau, Whitman, Melville, and Hawthorne. These men, as Mr. D. H. Lawrence has well said, reached a verge. They stood between two worlds. Part of their experience enabled them to bring the protestant movement to its conclusion: the critical examination of men, creeds, and institutions, which is the vital core of protestantism, could not go much further. But already, out of another part of their experience, that which arose out of free institutions planted in an unpreëmpted soil, molded by fresh contact with forest and sea and the more ingenious works of man, already this experience pushed them beyond the pit Melville fell into, and led them towards new institutions, a new art, a new philosophy, formed on the basis of a wider past than the European, caught by his Mediterranean or Palestinian cultures, was capable of seizing.

It was the organic break with Europe's past that enabled the American to go on; just as the immigration of people to America came to include specimens from almost all the folk of the world, so the American past widened sufficiently to bring Eastern and Western cultures into a common focus. The American went on. Whereas, in their search for a new basis for culture, Nietzsche went back to pre-Socratic Greece, Carlyle to Abbot Samson, Tolstoi and Dostoevsky to primitive Christianity, and Wagner to the early Germanic fables, Emerson, Thoreau, and Whitman went forward leaning on the experiences about them, using the past as the logger uses the corduroy road, to push further into the wilderness and still have a sound bottom under him. They fathomed the possibilities, these Americans, of a modern basis for culture, and fathoming it, were nearer to the sources of culture, nearer to the formative thinkers and poets of the past, than those who sought to restore the past. What is vital in the American writers of the Golden Day grew out of a life which opened up to them every part of their social heritage. And a thousand more experiences and fifty million more people have made us no wiser.

The spiritual fact remains unalterable, as Emerson said, by many or few particulars. It is the spiritual fact of American experience that we shall examine during the period of its clearest expression.

II

All the important thinkers who shared in this large experience were born between 1800 and 1820; their best work was done by the time the Civil War came; if not beyond the reach of its hurt, they at all events could not be completely overthrown or warped by it. The leader of these minds, the central figure of them all, was Ralph Waldo Emerson. He was the first American philosopher with a fresh doctrine: he was the first American poet with a fresh theme: he was the first American prose writer to escape, by way of the Elizabethan dramatists and the Seventeenth Century preachers, from the smooth prose of Addison or the stilted periods of Johnson. He was an original, in the sense that he was a source: he was the glacier that became the white mountain torrent of Thoreau, and expanded into the serene, ample-bosomed lake of Whitman. He loses a little by this icy centrality: he must be climbed, and there is so much of him that people become satisfied with a brief glimpse, and forget that they have not reached the summit which dominates the lower peaks and platforms. His very coldness seems familiar to academic minds; and for too long they appropriated him, as one of them: they forgot that his coldness is not that of an impotence, but of an inner intensity: it burns! The outward manner of his life was mild: there are summer afternoons when from the distance Mont Blanc itself seems little more than a cone of ice-cream; and his contemporaries forgot that this sweet man carried a lash, a lash that would not merely drive the money-changers from the temple but the priests.

Emerson was a sort of living essence. The preacher, the farmer, the scholar, the sturdy New England freeholder, yes, and the shrewd Yankee peddler or mechanic, were all encompassed by him; but what they meant in actual life had fallen away from him: he represented what they stood for in eternity. With Emerson's works one might reconstruct the landscape and society of New England: a few things would be left out from Nature which Thoreau would have to supply for us—a handful of flora and fauna, and the new Irish immigrants who were already building the railroads and who finally were to take possession of Boston—but what remained would still be everything of importance in the New England scheme of things. The weaknesses of New England are there, too: its bookishness, its failure, as Margaret Fuller said of Emerson, to kiss the earth sufficiently, its impatience to assume too quickly an upright position, its too-tidy moral house-keeping. Strong or weak, Emerson was complete: in his thought the potentialities of New England were finally expressed.

It is almost impossible to sum up Emerson's doctrine, for he touched life on many sides, and what is more, he touched it freshly, so though he is a Platonist, one will not find Plato's doctrines of Art in his essay on Art; and though he was in a very derivative way a Kantian, one will not find Kant's principles at the bottom of his ethics. With most of the resources of the past at his command, Emerson achieved naked-ness: his central doctrine is the virtue of this in-tellectual, or cultural, nakedness: the virtue of get-ting beyond the institution, the habit, the ritual, and finding out what it means afresh in one's own consciousness. Protestantism had dared to go this far with respect to certain minor aspects of the Catholic cult: Emerson applied the same method in a more sweeping way, and buoyed up by his faith in the future of America—a country endowed with perhaps every advantage except venerability—he asked not merely what Catholic ritual means, but all ritual, not merely what dynastic politics means but all politics; and so with every other important aspect of life. Emerson divested everything of its associations, and seized it afresh, to make what associations it could with the life he had lived and the experience he had assimilated. As a result, each part of the past came to him on equal terms: Buddha had perhaps as much to give as Christ: Hafiz could teach him as much as Shakespeare or Dante. Moreover, every fragment of present experience lost its associated values, too: towards the established hierarchy of experiences, with vested interests that no longer, perhaps, could exhibit the original power of sword or spade, he extended the democratic challenge: perhaps new experiences belonged to the summit of aristocracy, and old lines were dying out, or were already dead, leaving only empty venerated names.

Emerson saw the implications of this attempt to re-think life, and to accept only what was his. He did not shrink from them. "Nothing is at last sacred but the integrity of your own mind. . . . I remember an answer which when quite young I was prompted to make to a valued adviser, who was

wont to importune me with the dear old doctrines
of the church. On my saying, 'What have I to do
with the sacredness of traditions, if I live wholly
from within?' my friend suggested,—'But these impulses may be from below, not from above.' I re-
plied, ' They do not seem to me to be such; but if
I am the Devil's child, I will live then from the
Devil.' No law can be sacred to me but that of my
Nature."

"Life only avails, not the having lived." There
is the kernel of the Emersonian doctrine of self-re-
liance: it is the answer which the American, in the
day of his confidence and achievement, flung back
into the face of Europe, where the "having lived"
has always been so conspicuous and formidable. In
a certain sense, this doctrine was a barbarism; but
it was a creative barbarism, a barbarism that aimed
to use the old buildings not as a shell, but as a
quarry; neither casting them aside altogether, nor
attempting wretchedly to fit a new and lush existence into the old forms. The transcendental
young photographer, in Hawthorne's House of the
Seven Gables, suggested that houses should be built
afresh every generation, instead of lingering on in
dingy security, never really fitting the needs of any
family, but that which originally conceived and

built it. An uncreative age is aghast at this suggestion: for the new building may be cruder than the old, the new problem may not awaken sufficient creative capacities, equal to the previous one: these are the necessary counsels of prudence, impotence.

In the heyday of the American adventure, neither Emerson nor Hawthorne was afraid. Emerson rethought life, and in the mind he coined new shapes and images and institutions, ready to take the place of those he discarded. A building was perishable; a custom might fall into disuse; but what of it? The mind was inexhaustible; and it was only the unawakened and unimaginative practical people who did not feel that these dearly purchased trinkets might all be thrown into the melting pot and shaped over again, without a penny lost. It was not that nakedness itself was so desirable: but clothes were cheap! Why keep on piecing together and patching the old doctrines, when the supply never could run out, so long as life nourished Emersons? "We shall not always set so great a price," he exclaimed, "on a few texts, a few lives. We are like children who repeat by rote the sentences of grandames and tutors, and, as they grow older, of the men of talents and character they chance to see,—painfully recollecting the exact words they spoke; afterwards, when they come into the point of view which these had who uttered these sayings, they understand them, and are willing to let the words go; for at any time, they can use words as good when the occasion comes. . . . When we have new perceptions, we shall gladly disburden the memory of its hoarded treasures, as of old rubbish."

III

The Platonism of Emerson's mind has been over-emphasized; or rather, it has been misconstrued to mean that he lived in a perpetual cloud-world. The truth is, however, that Emerson's Platonism was not a matter simply of following Plato: it was a matter of living like Plato, and achieving a similar mode of thought. Critics have too often spoken of Plato's forms as if they were merely a weak escape from the urgent problems of Fifth-Century Athens; and of Emerson's, as if they were a neurotic withdrawal from the hurly-burly of American life. They were both, in a sense, a withdrawal; but it was a withdrawal of water into a reservoir, or of grain into a bin, so that they might be available later, if they could not be effectively distributed at once. Both Plato and Emerson had mixed with the life about them and knew its concrete details: both were conscious of the purely makeshift character of existing institutions; both were aware that they were in a period of transition. Instead of busying himself with the little details of political or economic readjustment, each sought to achieve a pattern which would permit the details to fall into place, and so make possible a creative renovation. Emerson wrote about Man the Reformer; but he never belonged to any political sect or cult. The blight of Negro slavery awakened his honest anger, and his essay on the Knownothings is an excellent diatribe: but even this great issue did not cause him to lose his perspective: he sought to abolish the white slaves who maintained that institution.

In coupling Emerson's name with Plato's I have hinted that Emerson was a philosopher; I see no reason to qualify this hint, or to apologize for the juxtaposition. He has been more or less grudgingly given such a place by current philosophic commentators, because on a superficial examination there is no originality in his metaphysics: both Plato and Kant had given an independent reality to the world of ideas, and the habit of treating existing facts as symbols is so ancient it became a shocking novelty when reëmployed in our own time by Dr. Sigmund

Freud. The bare metaphysical outlines of Emerson's work gives no insight, however, into the body of his thought as a whole. The contents of Emerson's philosophy is much richer, I think, than that of any of his contemporaries; and he is denied a high place in philosophy largely because the content is so rich that it cannot be recognized, in the attentuated twilight of academic groves, as philosophy. Hegel and Comte and Spencer, Emerson's contemporaries, had all found formulæ which led them into relations with a vast mass of concrete facts: the weakness of their several philosophies was due to severe defects of personality—they were sexually neurotic, like Comte, with his pathetic apotheosis of Clothilde, or they were querulous invalids, like Spencer, who had never been able to correct by a wider experience the original bias given to his mind by his early training as a railroad engineer. Emerson had the good fortune to live a healthy and symmetrical life: he answered Tolstoi's demand for essential greatness—he had no kinks. In him, philosophy resumed the full gamut of human experience it had known in Pythagoras and Plato.

Emerson's uniqueness, for his time, consists in the fact that he appreciated not merely the factual data of science, and the instrumental truth of sci-

entific investigation: he also recognized the formative rôle of ideas, and he saw the importance of
"dialectic" in placing new patterns before the mind
which did not exist, ready-made, in the order of
Nature. "All the facts of the animal economy, sex,
nutriment, gestation, birth, growth, are symbols of
the passage of the world into the soul of man, to
suffer there a change, and reappear a new and higher
fact." The occasion for, or the efficacy, of this
passage into the soul of man was denied by the externalism of Nineteenth Century empiricism; ob-
scurely, it was the ground for contention between
religion and science, a quarrel which religion lost by
holding fast to a purely superstitious empiricism.
If instrumental truths are the only order of truth,
all religion is a superstition, all poetry a puerility,
and all art itself is a weak anticipation of photog-
raphy and mechanical drawing.

Emerson's affirmation of both physics and dialectic, of both science and myth, an affirmation which
justified the existence of the artist, the poet, the
saint, was of prime importance; for he did not make
the mistake of disdaining the order and power that
science had achieved within its proper department.
Emerson was a Darwinist before the Origin of
Species was published, because he was familiar with

the investigations which were linking together the chain of organic continuity, and he was ready to follow the facts wherever they would lead him. Agassiz, Cambridge's great man of science, accepted the facts, too; but he was afraid of them; insulated in his evangelical Christianity, he insisted that the facts did not exist in Nature but in the mind of God. Emerson was untroubled by Agassiz's reluctance: the function of "God" was perpetually being performed for him in the passage of the world into the soul of man; and there was nothing in his philosophy to make him deny an orderly sequence in Nature. For Emerson, matter and spirit were not enemies in conflict: they were phases of man's experience: matter passed into spirit and became a symbol: spirit passed into matter and gave it a form; and symbols and forms were the essences through which man lived and fulfilled his proper being. Who was there among Emerson's contemporaries in the Nineteenth Century that was gifted with such a complete vision? To withhold the name of philosopher from the man who saw and expressed this integral vision of life so clearly is to deny the central office of philosophy.

Emerson's thought does not seal the world up into a few packets, tied with a formula, and place them in a pigeonhole. In the past, it was not limited to a phase of Christianity, nor a phase of classic culture: it roamed over a much wider area, and as he himself suggested, used Plato and Proclus, not for what they were, but as so many added colors for his palette. The past for Emerson was neither a prescription nor a burden: it was rather an esthetic experience. Being no longer inevitable in America, that is, no longer something handed down with a living at Corpus Christi or a place at court, the past could be entertained freely and experimentally. It could be revalued; and the paradox of Brahma became as acceptable as the paradox that the meek shall inherit the earth.

The poet, for Emerson, was the liberator; and in that sense, he was a great poet. With him one does not feel that our "civilization nears its meridian, but rather that we are yet only at the cock-crowing and the morning star." The promise of America, of an unspotted Nature and a fresh start, had seeped into every pore of Emerson's mind. "Do not set the least value on what I do," he warns, "nor the least discredit on what I do not, as if I pretended to settle anything as true or false. I unsettle all things. No facts to me are sacred; none are profane; I simply experiment, an endless seeker, with no Past at my back. . . . Why should we import rags and relics into the new hour? . . . Nothing is secure but life, transition, the energizing spirit. No love can be bound by oath or covenant to secure it against a higher love. No truth so sublime but it may be trivial to-morrow in the light of new thoughts. People wish to be settled: only as far as they are unsettled is there any hope for them."

The vigor of this challenge, the challenge of the American wilderness, the challenge of the new American society, where the European lost the security of his past in order to gain a better stake in the future—who but can feel that this is what was distinguished and interesting in our American experience, and what was salutary, for all its incidental defects, in the dumb physical bravado of the pioneer? Two men met the challenge and carried it further: Thoreau and Whitman. They completed the Emersonian circle, carrying the potted flower of the scholar's study out into the spring sunshine, the upturned earth, and the keen air.

THE DAWN

THE pioneer who broke the trail westward left scarcely a trace of his adventure in the mind: what remains are the tags of pioneer customs, and mere souvenirs of the past, like the Pittsburg stogy, which is our living connection to-day with the Connestoga wagon, whose drivers used to roll cigars as the first covered wagons plodded over the Alleghanies.

What the pioneer felt, if he felt anything, in the midst of these new solitudes; what he dreamt, if he dreamt anything; all these things we must surmise from a few snatches of song, from the commonplace reports issued as the trail was nearing its end, by the generation of Mark Twain and Hamlin Garland, or by the reflections of their sons and daughters, romantically eager, like John G. Neihardt's, critically reflective, like Susan Glaspell's, or wistfully sordid, like Edgar Lee Master's Anthology. Those who really faced the wilderness, and sought to make something out of it, remained in the East; in their reflection, one sees the reality that might have been. Henry David Thoreau was perhaps the only man who paused to give a report of the full experience. In a period when men were on the move, he remained still; when men were on the make, he remained poor; when civil disobedience broke out in the lawlessness of the cattle thief and the mining town rowdy, by sheer neglect, Thoreau practiced civil disobedience as a principle, in protest against the Mexican War, the Fugitive Slave Law, and slavery itself. Thoreau in his life and letters shows what the pioneer movement might have come to if this great migration had sought culture rather than material conquest, and an intensity of life, rather than mere extension over the continent.

Born in Concord about half a generation after Emerson, Thoreau found himself without the preliminary searchings and reachings of the young clergyman. He started from the point that his fellow-townsman, Emerson, had reached; and where the first cleared out of his mind every idea that made no direct connections with his personal experience, Thoreau cleared out of his life itself every custom or physical apparatus, to boot, which could not stand up and justify its existence. "A native of the United States," De Tocqueville had observed, "clings to the world's goods as if he were certain never to die; and he is so hasty at grasping at all within his reach, that one would suppose he was constantly afraid of not living long enough to enjoy them. He clutches everything, he holds nothing fast, but soon loosens his grasp to pursue fresh gratifications." Thoreau completely reversed this process: it was because he wanted to live fully that he turned away from everything that did not serve towards this end. He prized the minutes for what they brought, and would not exercise his citizenship at the town meeting, if a spring day by Walden Pond had greater promise; nor would he fill his hours with gainful practices, as a maker of pencils or a surveyor, beyond what was needed for the bare business of keeping his bodily self warm and active.

Thoreau seized the opportunity to consider what in its essentials a truly human life was; he sought, in Walden, to find out what degree of food, clothing, shelter, labor was necessary to sustain it. It was not animal hardihood or a merely tough physical regimen he was after; nor did he fancy, for all that he wrote in contempt of current civilization, that the condition of the woodcutter, the hunter, or the American Indian was in itself to be preferred. What he discovered was that people are so eager to get the ostentatious "necessaries" of a civil life that they lose the opportunity to profit by civilization itself: while their physical wants are complicated, their lives, culturally, are not enriched in proportion, but are rather pauperized and bleached.

Thoreau was completely oblivious to the dominant myths that had been bequeathed by the Seventeenth Century. Indifferent to the illusion of magnitude, he felt that Walden Pond, rightly viewed, was as vast as the ocean, and the woods and fields and swamps of Concord were as inexhaustible as the Dark Continent. In his study of Nature, he had recourse on occasion to the scientific botanists and zoölogists; but he himself had possession of a method that they were slow to arrive at; and it is easier for us to-day to understand the metaphysical distinction of Thoreau's kind of nature study than it would have been for Gray or Agassiz. Like Wordsworth before him, like Bergson after him, he realized that in current science "we murder to dissect," and he passed beyond the artful dismemberments of contemporary science to the flower and the bird and the habitat themselves. "Not a single scientific term or distinction," he wrote once in his notebook, "is the least to the purpose. You would fain perceive some-

thing and you must approach the object totally un-
prejudiced. You must be aware that nothing is
what you take it to be. . . . Your greatest success
will be simply to perceive that such things are, and
you will have no communication to make to the
Royal Society." In other words, Thoreau sought
in nature all the manifold qualities of being; he
was not merely in search of those likenesses or distinctions which help to create classified indexes and
build up a system. The esthetic qualities of a fern
were as important for his mode of apprehension as
the number of spores on a frond; it was not that he
disdained science, but that, like the old herbalists
and naturalists he admired, he would not let the
practical offices of science, its classification, its measurements, its numerations, take precedence over other
forms of understanding. Science, practiced in this
fashion, is truly part of a humane life, and a Darwin
dancing for joy over a slide in his microscope, or a
Pupin, finding the path to physics through his con-
templation of the stars he watched as a herd-boy
through the night, are not poorer scientists but
richer ones for these joys and delights: they merely
bow to the bias of utilitarianism when they leave
these things out of their reports. In his attitude
toward scientific truth Thoreau was perhaps a

prophetic figure; and a new age may do honor to his metaphysics as well as to his humanity.

The resolute acceptance of his immediate milieu as equal to the utmost that the earth could offer, stood by Thoreau in his other activities, too. He captained huckleberry parties as he might have led a battle, and was just as much the leader in one as he would have been in the other. His courage he reserved for better occasions than the battlefield, for he was ready to go to jail for his principles, and to mock Emerson for remaining outside. As for his country, he loved the land too well to confuse it with the shifting territorial boundaries of the National State. In this, he had that vital regional consciousness which every New Englander shared: Hawthorne himself had said that New England was as large a piece of territory as could claim his allegiance. Thoreau was not deceived by the rascality of politicians, who were ready to wage war for a coveted patch of Mexico's land; nor did he side with those who, for the sake of the Union, were ready to give up the principles that alone had made the Union valuable. What he loved was the landscape, his friends, and his companions in the spirit: when the Political State presumed to exercise a brass counter-claim on these loyalties it might go to the devil.

The Golden Day

Thoreau's attitude toward the State, one must note, was just the opposite to that of the progressive pioneer. The latter did not care what sort of landscape he "located" in, so long as he could salute the flag of his country and cast his vote: Thoreau, on the contrary, was far too religious a man to commit the idolatry of saluting a symbol of secular power; and he realized that the affairs controlled by the vote represented only a small fraction of an interesting life, while so far from being indifferent to the land itself, he absorbed it, as men have absorbed legends, and guarded it, as men preserve ceremonies. The things which his contemporaries took for the supreme realities of life, matter, money, and political rights, had only an instrumental use for Thoreau: they might contribute a little to the arrangement of a good life, but the good life itself was not contained, was not even implied in them. One might spend one's life pursuing them without having lived. "There is not one of my readers," he exclaimed, "who has yet lived a whole human life."

In Thoreau's time, industrialism had begun to puff itself up over its multiplication of goods and the increase of wants that it fostered, in order to provide the machine with an outlet for its ever-tooplentiful supply. Thoreau simply asked: "Shall we always study to obtain more of these things, and not sometimes be content with less?" "If we do not get our sleepers and forge rails and devote long days and nights to work," he observed ironically, "but go tinkering with our lives to improve *them*, who will build the railroads?" Thoreau was not a penurious fanatic, who sought to practice bare living merely as a moral exercise: he wanted to obey Emerson's dictum to save on the low levels and spend on the high ones. It is this that distinguishes him from the tedious people whose whole existence is absorbed in the practice of living on beans, or breathing deeply, or wearing clothes of a vegetable origin: simplification did not lead in Thoreau to the cult of simplicity: it led to a higher civilization.

What drove Thoreau to the solitude of the woods was no cynical contempt for the things beyond his reach. "Before we can adorn our houses with beautiful objects, the walls must be stripped, and our lives must be stripped, and beautiful housekeeping and beautiful living be laid for a foundation: now, a taste for the beautiful is most cultivated out of doors, where there is no house, and no housekeeper." The primeval woods were a favorable beginning for the search; but Thoreau did not think they could

be the end of it. The land itself, however, did stir
his imagination; he wrote:

All things invite this earth's inhabitants
To rear their lives to an unheard of height,
And meet the expectation of the land.

"The expectation of the land!" One comes upon
that phrase, or its equivalent, in almost every valid
piece of early American thought. One thinks of
moorland pastures by the sea, dark with bayberries
and sweet fern, breaking out among the lichened
rocks; and the tidal rivers bringing their weedy tang
to the low meadows, wide and open in the sun; the
purple pine groves, where the needles, bedded deep,
hum to the wind, or the knotted New England hills,
where the mountain laurel in June seems like upland
snow, left over, or where the marble breaks through
into clusters of perpetual laurel and everlasting;
one sees mountain lakes, giant aquamarines, sap-
phires, topazes, and upland pastures where the blue,
purple, lavender and green of the huckleberry bushes
give way in autumn to the fringe of sumach by the
roadside, volcanoes of reds and crimsons; the yel-
low of September cornfields, with intenser pumpkins
lying between the shocks, or the naked breasts and
flanks of the autumn landscape, quivering in uneasy

sleep before the white blanket puts it to rest. To smell this, taste this, and feel and climb and walk over this landscape, once untouched, like an unopened letter or a lover unkissed—who would not rise to meet the expectation of the land? Partly, it was the challenge of babyhood: how will it grow up and what will become of it? Partly, it was the charm of innocence; or again, it was the sense of the mighty variety that the whole continent gives, as if between the two oceans every possible human habitat might be built, and every conceivable variety of experience fathomed.

What the aboriginal Indian had absorbed from the young earth, Thoreau absorbed; what the new settlers had given her, the combing of the plow, the cincture of the stone fence or the row of planted elms, these things he absorbed too; for Thoreau, having tasted the settled life of Concord, knew that the wilderness was not a permanent home for man: one might go there for fortification, for a quickening of the senses, for a tightening of all the muscles; but that, like any retreat, is a special exercise and wants a special occasion: one returned to Nature in order to become, in a deeper sense, more cultivated and civilized, not in order to return to crudities that men had already discarded. Looking ahead, Thoreau saw what was needed to preserve the valuable heritage of the American wilderness. He wrote:

"The kings of England formerly had their forests to hold the king's game, for sport or food, sometimes destroying villages to create and extend them; and I think that they were impelled by a true instinct. Why should not we, who have renounced the king's authority, have our national preserves, where no villages need be destroyed, in which the bear and panther, and some even of the hunter race, may still exist, and not be 'civilized off the face of the earth,'—our own forests, not to hold the king's game merely, but to hold and preserve the king himself also, the lord of creation,—and not in idle sport of food, but for inspiration and our own true recreation? or shall we, like the villains, grub them all up, poaching on our own national domain?"

These pregnant suggestions of Thoreau, which were to be embodied only after two generations in our National and State Parks, and in projects like Mr. Benton Mackaye's great conception of the Appalachian trail, make the comments of those who see in him only an arch-individualist, half-Diogenes, half-Rousseau, seem a little beside the point. The individualism of an Emerson or a Thoreau was the

necessary complement of the thoroughly socialized
existence of the New England town; it was what
prevented these towns from becoming collections of
yes-men, with never an opinion or an emotion that
differed from their neighbors. He wrote for his
fellow-townsmen; and his notion of the good life
was one that should carry to a higher pitch the
existing polity and culture of Concord itself. "As
the nobleman of cultivated taste surrounds himself
with whatever conduces to his culture—genius—
learning—wit—books—paintings—statuary—music
philosophical instruments, and the like; so let the
village do—not stop short at a pedagogue, a par-
son, a sexton, a parish library, and three select-
men, because our pilgrim forefathers got through a
cold winter once on a bleak rock with these. To
act collectively is according to the spirit of our
institutions; and I am confident that, as our circumstances are more flourishing, our means are greater
than the nobleman's." Do not those sentences alter
a little our stereotype of homespun New England,
of Individualistic America?

Just as Thoreau sought Nature, in order to arrive
at a higher state of culture, so he practiced individualism, in order to create a better order of
society. Taking America as it was, Thoreau con-

ceived a form, a habitat, which would retain what
was unique in the American contact with the virgin
forest, the cultivated soil, and the renewed institutions of the New England town. He understood
the precise thing that the pioneer lacked. The
pioneer had exhausted himself in a senseless external
activity, which answered no inner demands except
those for oblivion. In his experiment at Walden
Pond, Thoreau "learned this, at least . . . that if
one advances confidently in the direction of his
dreams, and endeavors to live the life which he has
imagined, he will meet with success unexpected in
the common hours. . . . In proportion as he sim-
plifies his life, the laws of the universe will appear
less complex, and solitude will not be solitude, nor
poverty poverty, nor weakness weakness. If you
have built castles in the air, your work need not be
lost; that is where they should be. Now put the
foundations under them."

In short, Thoreau lived in his desires; in rational
and beautiful things that he imagined worth doing,
and did. The pioneer lived only in extraneous necessities; and he vanished with their satisfaction: filling
all the conditions of his environment, he never fulfilled himself. With the same common ground between them in their initial feeling towards Nature,

Thoreau and the pioneer stood at opposite corners of the field. What Thoreau left behind is still precious; men may still go out and make over America in the image of Thoreau. What the pioneer left behind, alas! was only the burden of a vacant life.

▼

HIGH NOON

"HE that by me spreads a wider breast than my own proves the width of my own." So Walt Whitman chanted in the Song of Myself; and in the greatness of Whitman the genius of Emerson was justified. Walt Whitman was a cosmos: he was inclusive where Emerson and Thoreau were restrictive: he was sensual and jolly where they were refined and taut: he identified himself with the mere bulk and vastness of the American continent, and, with a tremendous appetite for the actual, entered into the experience of the pioneer, the roadhand, the mechanic, the woodman, the soldier, the farmer. In some remote Dutch ancestor of Whitman's one figures the men and women of Franz Hals's portraiture, people large, lusty, loving, men who like their sweetheart and their steak, women who give themselves to love as the flower bows to the weight of the bee. With Emerson, to repeat the obvious, one surveys the world from a glacial summit: the air is rarefied, and at the distance even the treacherous places in the landscape seem orderly and innocent. With Whitman one sees the heights from the bosom of the valley: the "unseen is proved by the seen, till that becomes unseen, and receives proofs of its own."

Whitman absorbed so much of the America about him, that he is more than a single writer: he is almost a literature. Pushing his way like some larval creature through one husk after another, through the hard shell of Puritanism, in which he wrote Temperance Tracts, through the shell of republicanism in which he glorified all the new political institutions, through the flimsy casement of romantic poetry, iridescent with cheap colors and empty rhymes, Whitman finally achieved his own metamorphosis, and emerged, with dripping wings, into the untempered mid-day of the American scene. The stages of this metamorphosis have created contradictions in Whitman's work; and if we are to appreciate his full achievement, we must be ready to throw aside the vestiges of his larval state.

First, there was in Whitman a certain measure of the political religiosity of Joel Barlow and Philip Freneau. Political nationalism, in certain aspects of Whitman's thought, assumed a mystical beauty and centrality: he wrote about the United States

as if they were the tissue of men's eternal desires—
as if the robbery of Mexican territory, for example,
could be justified to the Mexicans as well as the
Americans by the inevitable drag of our Manifest
Destiny. Here Whitman was confusing spiritual
with temporal dominion. He had conceived new
spiritual patterns, appropriate to the modern,
which were to be fulfilled in the America of his
dreams; and it was hard to resist identifying this
hope of a wider America with the expansionist
activities of political bandits. In this mood, to
speak frankly, Whitman ranted.

Nevertheless, when one sums up Whitman's observations upon the Union and upon the political
state of the country, no one surely ever ranted with
so many reservations; and it is unfair to take the
bombastic lines out of the context that perpetually
qualifies them. The political reality that was so
precious to Whitman was only a means of permitting the growth of "superb persons," and a life,
"copious, vehement, spiritual, bold." Moreover, between the Walt Whitman who wrote the original
Leaves of Grass, and the defeated and paralyzed
man who lingered on through the Gilded Age, there
is a difference; and by 1879 Whitman had come to
realize that his democracy was one that had been

based on free land and equal opportunity to use it, and that failure was beginning to threaten the political structure. "If the United States," he wrote, "like the countries of the Old World, are also to grow vast crops of poor, desperate, dissatisfied, nomadic, miserably waged populations, such as we see looming upon us of late years—steadily, even if slowly, eating into them like a cancer of lungs or stomach—then our republican experiment, notwithstanding all its surface-successes, is at heart an unhealthy failure. . . ." That was not all. "By the unprecedented open-up of humanity enmasse in the United States in the last hundred years, under our institutions, not only the good qualities of the race, but just as much the bad ones, are prominently brought forward. Man is about the same, in the main, whether with despotism or whether with freedom."

That saving and irrefragable common sense was what ballasted all of Whitman's hopes and expectations. He lived to see the America he dreamed of undermined and rotten: he saw the Kings of Iron and Oil and Cotton supplant not merely the older ones who ruled by divine right but the new one elected quadrennially by the people: he saw the diverse but well-mixed America of his youth give way

to the America of the melting pot, which neither
welded the old nationalities nor had the spiritual
power to create a new one: he saw the sickly barbers
and perfumers of the New York literary schools of
the forties turn into the gentlemanly tailors who
cut their stories and their thoughts to fit the fat
paunches of the middle classes in the seventies: he
saw all this, and denied nothing. No critic ferreted
out the weaknesses and pettinesses of America with
a surer nose than Whitman tracked them down in
his Democratic Vistas: what could be said against
his dream, Whitman said, with the staunch candor
of a friend. But his thought and his vision were
unshaken; the promise of America had not disappeared. If it was absent from the immediate
scene, it had nevertheless taken form in his poems;
and his poems were still waiting to shape a new
America.

In Leaves of Grass Whitman had fulfilled Emerson
in more ways than either of them suspected. There
are passages of Emerson's prose which have, poten-
tially, the prosody of Whitman; but whereas Emerson's poems, at their best, remain fragmentary and
broken, because the meaning was somehow always
warping the metes and measures Emerson respected
and clung to, in Whitman, at his best, these new

thoughts find their own beat, and become poetry of
the first rank. Whitman had discovered Emerson's
inner form in creating his own. He himself had
stammered and stuttered so long as he kept to the
old metres: his early work was weak and sentimental
because he had nothing to say within the bounds of
those previous culture-molds which Whitman tagged
as "feudal." New streams of thought and experience were confluent in Whitman: the *Weltanschauung*
of Hegel, precursor of the evolutionists, who saw
the world as a continual becoming, and both the
bad and the good as part of the total meaning of
the universe; the electric doctrine of Emerson, which
bade every man find his own center and every institution to answer up for its results in one's own life;
the unstratified society of America, where the bus
driver was as good as the next man, and the private
soldier as great as the statesman whose policies
reduced him to a pawn; the cleansing operations of
science, which confronted every variety in thought,
and made no more distinction between the clean and
the unclean, the minute and the immense, than some
indifferent deity, for whom the fall of a gnat and
the fall of an Empire are of precisely the same importance. Out of the discussions of the Fourierists,
and the societies of Free Lovers, and women who

pressed for the political and social emancipation of
their sex, as well as out of his own capacious adventures, Whitman got the courage to deal with the
varieties of sexual experience, too: in the Children
of Adam and Calamus he brushed past the nice
restraints of Emerson—who "held his nose" at its
passages—and Thoreau, who, like Natty Bumpo
and Paul Bunyan, averted himself from any passion
more intense than friendship.

Whitman took in the quaker, the puritan, the cosmopolitan, the pioneer, the republican; and what
came out in his poems was none of these things: it
was a new essence; none of the ordinary labels
described it. It had the smell of reality which was
science; it had the largeness of comprehension
which was philosophy; and it had the doubts, searchings, quests, achievements, and consummations which
are the stuff of life itself. Whitman found no need
to add an extra dimension to his experience: to
transcribe for him was in the highest sense to
translate. Whatever tended to create full-bodied
and full-minded men and women tended toward en-
larging the significance of every single activity, no
matter how base or minute. The veil of appearance
was as mysterious and beautiful as anything behind
the veil. Perhaps it was all Maya, all illusion; or

perhaps life was like a set of Chinese boxes: one removed the outer box of appearance, and discovered another box—appearance. What of it? A single blade of grass was enough to confound all the atheists; and whatever else the universe might hold, he reckoned that there was no sweeter meat than that which clung to his own bones. Such faith does not need external props and certitudes: it mocks at the testimony of bibles, for it is itself the source of such testimony.

People have hesitated to call Whitman's poems poetry; it is useless to deny that they belong to sacred literature. If the Leaves of Grass are not poetry, it is only because not every generation endows us with such a poet.

VI

Literature may be evocative or formative: one plays upon sentiments, emotions, ideas that already exist: the other changes the very attitude of the audience, and calls new ones forth. The common American of the Golden Day responded to Longfellow and Whittier; for these men caught his ordinary mood, measured off and rhymed; and even when Whittier and Lowell wrote on abolition themes, they

were only touching strings which a Garrison or a
Wendell Phillips had already set in motion. It is
amusing to note the way in which ante-bellum America responded to Whitman. Emerson and Thoreau
were quick to see his genius, even to proclaim it.
Lesser people, however, like Moncure Conway, were
a little disappointed in him: they expected to find
in Whitman the common workman, grown vocal,
some one who could be taken into society and
patronized; some one who would bolster up their
notion of a poet who had risen from the lowly ranks.

Whitman was not a democrat, in the sense of
being a popular mediocrity; he was a man of genius;
who, mid all his school teaching, editing, carpenter-
ing, type-setting and what-not remained consecrated
to the profession of letters: Jesus of Sirach was no
more certain of his vocation. Whitman was
Pygmalion to his own Galatea: he had formed himself, so that he might give a new model to America.
The imperturbable landscape, the satisfaction and
aplomb of animals, the ecstasy of hearty lovers, the
meditations of one who sits withdrawn in the crowd,
or on a mountain top—Whitman extracted from
these things a new shape, which was himself. Every
poem of Whitman's is the man; every part of the
man threw forth tendrils which clung to the objects

of poems. One could not become a sympathetic reader of Whitman without re-forming oneself into an approximation of this new shape. Only commonplace works of art reflect the everyday personality of the reader: the supreme works always show or hint of the new shape the reader may become: they are prophetic, formative. One might remove Longfellow without changing a single possibility of American life; had Whitman died in the cradle, however, the possibilities of American life would have been definitely impoverished. He created a new pattern of experience and character. The work he conceived still remains to be done: the America he evoked does not as yet exist.

Whitman was a poet in the braid Scots sense of makkar: a maker or creator. He was conscious of the fact that the accumulated culture of Europe had lost a good part of its original meaning, through lack of direct contact with the new forces of discovery, science, democracy: the work of the old makkars was crumbling away; at best, it was repeated by rote, as in the churches, without any sense of the living reality, or the finer passages were rolled on the tongue, for sensation's sake, by an aristocratic minority. "Note to-day," Whitman observed in Democratic Vistas, "a curious spectacle

and conflict. . . . Science, testing absolutely all
thoughts, all works, has already burst well upon the
world—a sun, mounting, most illuminating, most
glorious, surely never again to set. But against it,
deeply entrenched, holding possession, yet remains
(not only through the churches and schools but by
imaginative literature and unregenerate poetry) the
fossil theology of the mythic-materialistic superstitious, untaught and credulous, fable-loving primitive ages of humanity."

Whitman saw that the office of sacred literature ✓
was no longer being performed; or at all events,
that those who were pursuing it were not fully conscious of either the need or the opportunity.
Vulgar literature was, indeed, growing hugely.
"To-day, in books, in the rivalry of writers, especially novelists, success (so-called) is for him or
her who strikes the mean flat average, the sensational
appetite for stimulus, incident, persiflage, etc., and
depicts to the common caliber, sensual, exterior life."
What remained of sacred literature was insufficient
to offset this. It was to establish a central point in
literature, in terms of science and the modern, that
Whitman created: American poetry was to do in
our day what the Vedas, the Nackas, the Talmud,
the Old Testament, the Gospel, Plato's works had

done for their time: it was to crystallize our most precious experience and in turn to modify, by that act of crystallization, the daily routine.

What, in fact, were the active formative literatures when Whitman wrote? In the Western World the principal one was, without doubt, that great miscellany called the Old Testament, supplemented by the gospels; and among the cultivated classes, Homer, Horace, Plutarch, Dante, Shakespeare, Corneille, played a lively but minor part. The Romantic movement, which went back to the ballads and the folk-literature of the various regions of Europe was a recognition of the fact that something was lacking in both the Hebrew and the classic traditions, and in the literature which was directly founded upon them. What was lacking was the direct historic connection with a people, a place, and a special way of life. It is true that all literature has certain common characters, and no great works of the spirit are foreign and remote; but, as Whitman pointed out, "something is rooted in the invisible roots, the profoundest meanings, of a place, race, or nationality," and the Romantic movement had cut loose from classic and Hebraic influences in order to absorb this more intimate order of meaning and find a nearer and fresher source of spiritual activity. Blake, Keats, Shelley, had partly achieved this; Wordsworth alone, however, had created new forms without relying on a mythic-materialistic past.

With what was universal in all these efforts, Whitman could sympathize: Homer and Shakespeare and the Bible had been his daily food. He sought to do for common men and women, for the contemporary and the ordinary-heroic, what Shakespeare had achieved in his great images of the aristocratic life. In America, in modern life, on the farm and in the laboratory, in the progress of souls along the grand roads of the Universe, in company with the Great Companions, the swift and majestic men, the capacious and broad-bosomed women—here was the stuff for new Vedas, Cycles, and Testaments. Whitman overvalued, if anything, the contrivances of political democracy; but that was only a first step; he overcountenanced, if anything, the absorption of America in materialistic effort; that, however, was only the second step. Neither political democracy nor industrial progress were for him anything but a prelude to the third stage, rising out of the two previous ones, and creating a "native expression spirit" and an abundance of rich personalities.

In his effort to keep ballasted and always find a landing place in contemporary existence, Whitman was perhaps too receptive and undiscriminating in his acknowledgement of current values and aims; in his old age, he accepted with child-like delight the evidences of material prosperity he found on his Western trip. His Hegelianism was dangerous stuff: it lead him to identify the Real and the Ideal, instead of seeing, as William James put it, that they were dynamically continuous. But at the core, Whitman was never deceived: he knew that the meaning of all current activity lay only in the forms or symbols it created and the rational purposes it embodied; and so far from believing that the work of the poet or artist would be supplanted by science, he believed that "the highest and subtlest and broadest truths of modern science wait for their true assignment and last vivid flashes of light—as Democracy waits for its—through first-class metaphysicians and speculative philosophs—laying the basements and foundations for these new, more expanded, more harmonious, more melodious, freer American poems." To indicate these new meanings, to open up these new relationships, Whitman wrote his poems. I can think of no one in whom the unconscious and the conscious process worked more in harmony: the life and the doctrine were one. So far as Whitman went, he achieved his end.

So far as he went! Most people are unaware that the Leaves of Grass, Calamus, the Children of Adam, are only a part of the vast canvas he projected; they do not realize that he was diverted from his original intention and never lived to complete it. The Leaves of Grass were to deal chiefly with the palpable and the material; there was to be a complementary volume which would center mainly on the spiritual and the inactual—upon death and immortality and final meanings—for he was the poet of the body and he was the poet of the soul. Alas! the Civil War came. He threw himself into it as a hospital visitor, giving his personality and his radiant health to the sick and the wounded, as these men had given themselves in the camp and on the battlefield. Within a few years this ordeal exacted its revenge: he became paralyzed, and as he never fully recovered his physical powers, his mental powers diminished, too: if they are still at their summit in Drum-Taps, they recurred only fitfully in the later poems: and though he could outline his aspiration with a firm hand in Democratic Vistas, published in 1871, he could no longer model it and round it out. What he meant to create is implied in all his poems; the whole of it was never, perhaps, expressed.

Whitman himself had felt that the War for the American Union was the Odyssey of his generation; but except for himself and Herman Melville, no one lived to write about it in those terms; the stories of Ambrose Bierce, Stephen Crane, and Upton Sinclair did not treat it in this vein. Whitman did not see that the great conflict might have a Punic ending. As it turned out, the war was a struggle between two forms of servitude, the slave and the machine. The machine won, and the human spirit was almost as much paralyzed by the victory as it would have been by the defeat. An industrial transformation took place over night: machines were applied to agriculture; they produced new guns and armaments; the factory regime, growing tumultuously in the Eastern cities, steadily undermined the balanced regimen of agriculture and industry which characterized the East before the war.

The machines won; and the war kept on. Its casualties were not always buried at Antietam or Gettysburg; they moldered, too, in libraries, studies, offices. The justifiable ante-bellum optimism of Emerson turned into a waxen smile. Whitman lost his full powers in what should have been his prime.

Among the young men, many a corpse was left, to go through the routine of living. But before the Golden Day was over, the American mind had lived through a somber and beautiful hour, the hour of Hawthorne and Melville. With them, the sun turned to a candle, and cast black shadows upon the wall, not the empty grotesque shadows of Poe, but the shapes of a magnified if distorted humanity.

TWILIGHT

HAWTHORNE was the afterglow of the Seventeenth Century. With him came the twilight of Puritanism as a spiritual force. Presently, it became altogether a handy servant of industry, and as a system of ideas, ceased to be interesting or to attract interesting minds. Men like Josiah Royce, born some fifty years after Hawthorne, became, in the jargon of philosophy, absolute idealists; those who did not take this path, flourished in negations. Puritanism left its mark on America after the Civil War chiefly through its code of inhibitions and avoidances; in this sense, it is still with us. In Hawthorne, however, the conviction which produced a Paradise Lost or a Pilgrim's Progress still glowed with a white intensity; but its heat was gone. Hawthorne was silver; the silver of moonlight; the silver of fine goblets; the tarnished silver of ancient and abandoned houses, locked in moldy drawers.

Hawthorne was no longer frightened by the

bogies of the Puritan hell; but his interest in human weakness and its consequences remained: he was an esthetician of sin. Into the shadows of Seventeenth Century New England, with a consciousness that remained outwardly Puritan, he projected the figures of his own day. One does not perhaps recognize in the Scarlet Letter and in The House of the Seven Gables the torments of the modern consciousness; but they are there. Pull off the costumes and look closely at these Hesters and Hepzibahs: they are sisters of the Annas and Nastasyas that the great Russians are portraying. Did you think that the Scarlet Letter was placed upon the waxen breast of a dummy? Do not be deceived. The flesh is tender, and the heart beats. The characters in Hawthorne's principal tragedy were both symbolic and real: Chillingworth was a vengeful, impotent old man: he was also a deterministic Puritanism, caught within its materialist circle, and unable to take possession of life, to which it had been too lately and grudgingly wedded. The young minister was a sweet, neurotic soul, impotent through conflict, where Chillingworth was impotent through denial: he was the prototype of the Ruskins and Amiels who haunted the century: he was likewise the figure of a weak and spindly idealism which faints at the first

warm breath of reality, and dare not acknowledge
the child it has begotten. Hester need not forfeit
her own existence to become the creative spirit itself,
breaking away from the Puritanic bond, unsatisfied
by the temporary union with Transcendentalism—
it did not take Hawthorne long to discover the in-
sufficiency of Brook Farm—and living out, with a
single child, a destiny without husband or lover.

I have perhaps read too freely into the fable:
Hawthorne himself had no such conscious purpose
as that I have been trying to explicate: but the novel
will bear pondering: it is no mere study of the
external rigors of an abandoned creed. If I err,
I am absurd in the same way that Hawthorne himself was, when he made a note of a gas main that lay
beneath a whole city, and wondered whether it might
not be made the symbol of some widespread but
secret evil. At heart, the American novelists were
all transcendental. The scene was a symbol: they
scarcely had the patience to describe it: they were
interested in it only because it pointed to something
more important. Even Poe, who sneered at Concord, was equally an imaginative Transcendentalist:
Mardi and the Fall of the House of Usher, and the
Scarlet Letter were all of one brood. These writers

were lost in the inactual: sin, death, eternity—these held their minds, not "chops and tomato sauce"!

There is a tragic moment in all experience, which good health cannot overcome, which good institutions cannot avert. Hawthorne was conscious of this inescapable thread of evil, and delighted in the complicated arabesque it presents to the mind when traced over the whole tapestry of existence. Sometimes the evil appeared to him as heredity, as it does with the Jews; sometimes it is fate, more dumb and irremediable—a life which has not faced this lurking and inscrutable malevolence has only made a childish reckoning of its possibilities. Hawthorne followed its last intricacy with the patience of a physiologist lingering over a microscopic slide of morbid tissue. What could the professional optimists make of this doctrine? Was it not just the clammy perspiration left on the walls of old New England buildings? Would it not be removed by central heating, a fresh coat of paint, or some other external improvement? Who could believe that life presented inherent evils which no mechanical improvements would diminish: who dared to believe this as long as the population of New Eden doubled every five years, and real-estate values kept going up?

The possibilities of tragic experience in America

were passing away, even when Hawthorne was writing. There was no tragedy in the program of the pioneer and the industrialist: there was just success or disappointment, whereas tragedy shows the canker that rots success, and the depth of a sorrow that belittles disappointment; doing so, it summons up that greatness of spirit in which Hester, for example, faces life, once her most painful part has been acted out. There is no surer test of the quality of life in what I have called the Golden Day, than the two tragedies, The Scarlet Letter and Moby Dick, which issued out of it. The sunlight had in Emerson and Whitman penetrated to every spot, and in its presence, the dark corners became more intense. If one explored the white summits of the glacier with Emerson, one might also fall into the abyss with Melville. One climbed high; and when one fell, the fall was deep.

VIII

The waters that unite the continents of the world once meant more to the thin strip of communities that lined that Atlantic coast than the prairies where the buffalo wandered. Sloops and catboats plied the inlets and the rivers, bungs and schooners

went up and down the coast; and at last, after a
hundred years of boat-building, the clipper-ship,
designed in the shipyards of New York and Boston
and Newburyport and Portland, began to scud
dangerously over the seas, carrying ice cut during
the winter on Walden Pond or Fresh Pond to cool
the merchant of Calcutta, picking up cargoes of
teas and silks, or venturing out from Long Island
or New Bedford, to stay years on the water in pursuit of the whale.

A lad leaves his schoolmates, and at twenty navi-
gates his father's ship; a girl sails with her husband,
nurses him during a difficult illness, and brings the
ship safely to port, making all the reckonings herself; in the long watches, as the ship sails on even
keel, the mind is open to new thoughts and fresh
insights: Morse invents his telegraph aboard ship,
and Colt makes a wooden model of the deadly
revolver: those who are more reflective than ingenious mix their thoughts with adventure and derring-do: a ship opens the mind of a young lawyer
named Dana, and it never opens so satisfactorily
again: life on board ship is the beginning of Henry
George's intellectual adventure.

Every year these quiet inlets launched their ships;
the clipper was the supreme esthetic achievement of

the day and land, better by far than current architecture or painting; and, unlike the covered wagon, these vessels returned. On board and in port, the beauty and brutality of the life mingled, the strength and the arrogance and the hardness and whipcord skill, the bullying, the petty meanness, the greed, the concupiscence, the fierce press of work in a storm contrasted with the occasions of sweet profound apathy, the immensity of quiet nights under the stars, and the hot pressure of strange courtesans, flagrant with perfumes, in the little houses one might stumble upon in the bazaars of Colombo or Canton. Put all this over against the measured, fussy life of New York or Baltimore, respectable, sensible, at bottom banal and sordid. Such heights and such depths! He who had touched them knew too well that no mean could be golden!

Herman Melville, born in New York in the same year as Whitman, mixed of the same Dutch-English stock, dying, too, within a year of Whitman, Herman Melville turned to the sea, and, in the great age of our seamanship, tasted for himself the qualities of both Odysseus and Homer. From his personal adventures, after he had jumped ship in the South Seas, he wrote that fine idyll of the tropics called Typee. Face to face with the savages of the

Marquesas, he discovered that in mere joyousness
of life, civilization had nothing to endow a man with
that these ferocious and innocent cannibals did not
possess: on the contrary, considered merely as animal existence, there was a more beautiful and
exuberant animality in the savage state than in the
hard pragmatic routine of our urban money-
warrens. While he stuck to the sea, the whaler, the
merchantman, and the man-of-war each made their
contribution to Melville. Finally, at the age of
thirty, he gathered himself for a great effort: the
result was the epic poem called Moby Dick.

The quality of Moby Dick and the fate of Moby
Dick throw an interesting light upon the cast of
mind that characterized the age. After the usual
brief success Melville's books almost all enjoyed, it
was tossed aside, to eke out an existence as a boy's
book of adventure. Swift's satire had met the same
fate, and for the same reason: adults who wish to
prolong their infantile state turn books like this
over to children upon whom the deeper fable can
make no impression, whilst they themselves take comfort in books that are written out of a more puerile
consciousness. That Moby Dick was not recognized,
except here and there by an isolated critic, as a
great book, is due to the fact, I think, that Moby

Dick is poetry. The jolly and comfortable bourgeois tradition of the Victorian age, a state of mind
composed of felt slippers and warm bellywash, could
not produce such a work: the genius of its great
writers, its Dickenses and Thackerays, was of quite
another cut. To find a parallel for Moby Dick one
must go back to Dekker, Heywood, Webster, Mar-
lowe, and Thomas Browne; men who translated the
drab events of the outer life into a wild and passionate dialect of their own. These are the kin of Melville. His prose, too, had the richness of the early
Seventeenth Century, capable of great rhythms,
always ready to float easily off the sandbars of commonplace description and out onto the rolling waters
of the grand style. In Whitman and Melville letters
again became as racy as the jabber of a waterside
saloon; in all of Poe's poetry there is scarcely a line
as good as pages of the best of Melville's prose.

Moby Dick was not merely poetry; it was a product of that deep meditation on the world and life and
time which makes philosophy; and among the treasures of the book is a single paragraph which might
claim a place beside whole treatises on the central
problems of destiny, fate, free-will. I cannot for-
bear putting it down. It takes rise from an after-
noon on which Melville was calmly performing one

of the routine functions of the ship, the making of a mat.

"As I kept on passing and repassing the filling or woof of marline between the long yarns of the warp, using my hand for the shuttle . . . it seemed as if this were the Loom of Time, and I myself were a shuttle mechanically weaving away at the Fates. There lay the fixed threads of the warp subject to but one single, ever-returning, unceasing vibration, and that vibration merely enough to admit of the crosswise interbinding of other threads with its own. The warp seemed necessity, and here, thought I, with my own hand I ply my own shuttle and weave my own destiny into these unalterable threads. Meantime, Queequeg's impulsive, indifferent sword, sometimes hitting the woof slantingly, or crookedly, or strongly, or weakly, as the case might be; and by this difference in the concluding blow producing a corresponding contrast in the final aspect of the completed fabric; this savage's sword, thought I, which thus finally shapes and fashions both warp and woof; this easy, indifferent sword must be chance—aye, chance, free will, and necessity—nowise incompatible—all interweavingly working together. The straight warp of necessity, not to be swerved from its ultimate course—its ever alternating vibration, indeed, only tending to that; free will still free to ply the shuttle between given threads; and chance, though restricted in its play within the right lines of necessity, and sideways in its motions directed by free will, though thus prescribed to by both, chance by turn rules either, and has the last featuring blow at events."

If this generation did not produce any skilled professional philosophers, I am not sure that it altogether lacked the living stuff of philosophy.

Melville, who was a friend and neighbor of Hawthorne in the Berkshires, once wrote into an enthusiastic description of Hawthorne's work a true picture of his own. "There is a certain tragic phase of humanity which, in our opinion, was never more powerfully embodied than by Hawthorne. We mean the tragedies of human thought in its own unbiased, native, and profounder working. We think that in no recorded mind has the intense feeling of the useable truth ever entered more deeply than into this man's by useable truth we mean the apprehension of the absolute condition of present things as they strike the eye of the man who fears them not, though they do their worst to him,—the man who . . . declares himself a sovereign nature in himself, amid the powers of heaven, hell, and earth. He may perish but so long as he exists he insists upon treating with all powers upon an equal basis."

The absolute condition of present things was what Melville sought to track down in the fable and the myth of the White Whale. One may read Moby Dick as a story of the sea, and be irritated by the lengthy description of whales and whaling; one may read it as a treatise on the whaling industry, and be irritated by the irrelevant heroic figure of Ahab, or the innocent sinister beauty of Queequeeg; and since it is also this, one may read it as an epic of the human spirit, and discover an equivalent of its symbolism in one's own consciousness. For me, the Whale is Nature, the Nature man warily hunts and subdues, the Nature he captures, tethers to his ship, cuts apart, scientifically analyzes, melts down, uses for light and nourishment, sells in the market, the Nature that serves man's purposes so long as he uses his wits and can ride on top. But with all this easy adventuring, there is another and deadlier Nature—the White Whale—a Nature that threatens man and calls forth all his heroic powers, and in the end defeats him with a final lash of the tail. That part of Nature cannot be harpooned, cannot be captured, still less drawn and quartered and sold. In sheer savagery—or was it perhaps in play?—

the White Whale had once amputated Ahab's leg: with relentless vigilance Ahab follows the White Whale to its lair, impatient of baser catches on the way, as the great philosophers and poets have been impatient of the little harpoonings and dickerings of science and the practical life. The White Whale is not the kindly, milk-fed Absolute, in which all conflicts are reconciled and all contradictions united into a higher kind of knowledge; no, the White Whale is the sheer brute energy of the universe, which challenges and checks the spirit of man. It is only the lonely heroic spirit, who declares himself a sovereign nature, that dares follow the White Whale; and once he comes to close quarters with the creature, there is no issue but death. The White Whale is the external force of Nature and Destiny. In the end it conquers: it must conquer: until the spirit of man is itself Leviathan, and can meet its antagonist on even terms.

In Moby Dick Melville carried the private voyage of the soul to its inevitable conclusion. Men are sustained, in faith and work, not by what they find in the universe, but by what man has built there. Man gave the word: he gave the symbol: he gave the form: he believed in his ejaculations and created language; he believed in his forms and wrought cities: he believed in his symbols, and created myth, poetry, science, philosophy. Deny this initial act of faith, tear aside the veil man has thrown between his own experience and the blank reality of the universe and everything else becomes meaningless: depend upon one's private self alone and though the renunciation be heroic, the result is inevitable: the White Whale will swallow one at a gulp. To appreciate the reality of the White Whale is to see more deeply into the expedience of all our intermediate institutions, all the spiritual shelters man puts between himself and the uncertain cosmic weather. Meaning, significance, attends only that little part of the universe man has built up and settled; the South Sea Islander, in his lazy and primitive culture, had achieved this meaning and lived happily; Melville, having divested himself of the meanings man had wrought and faced the universe as a sovereign power was confronted by a blank: he peered behind the curtain, and heard the dim rattle of his breath echoing through the abyss: nothing was there! So far can the spirit go by itself; no farther. If it returns at all, it is back to the common life.

On the imaginative level of Moby Dick Melville never again walked: he had exhausted himself. In his short-stories, he pictured himself more than once as an old man; and at thirty he was already that. There are tortured fragments of Melville in Mardi and Pierre; but the depth and bottom of the man had been sounded in Moby Dick. From that time on he lived in a sort of mechanical dream. His marriage, his wandering through the Near East, his interest in the Civil War—none of these could heal his spirit. He succumbed to rheumatism and the burden of supporting his family; the greater part of his manhood he clung tenaciously, like a ghost rattling his chains, to the post in the Customs House at Gansevoort Street. Fame, ambitions, friends, travel, love, nothing was left him in all this; he had exhausted their possibilities before he was thirty-five.

For thirty years Melville was like the dead man of Poe's, whose processes of decomposition were halted. He died twice: nothing in the drab and dapper America after the Civil War could recall him to the advantages of an earthly existence. The forms and activities of the new day—what were they? Could he look upon Howells as his son; could he treat Mark Twain as an equal? "Life," Hawthorne had written, "is made up of marble and mud." Melville, who had so superbly shaped the marble, was unable to do anything with the mud, or rather, he let the mud overwhelm him, and sank into it deeper and deeper. The American had faced the tragedy of the White Whale. He was now to retire to nearer and shallower waters. Emerson, Thoreau, Whitman, Melville, yes, and Hawthorne had answered the challenge of American experience. Presently, their heroic words will be forgotten, and their successors, living corpses, too, will look back to the days of their youth, as to a dream, real only while it lasted.

CHAPTER FOUR

THE PRAGMATIC ACQUIESCENCE

THE Civil War arose in a mess of muddy issues. The abolitionists' attack upon slavery, full of moral righteousness and oblivious to the new varieties of slavery that were being practiced under industrialism, stiffened the South into a spasm even more self-righteous, even more blind. Twenty years of fierce debate found the Southerner frequently denying that the Negro was a human being: it also found the abolitionist denying that the slaveholder was a human being. In that temper, all the rational humane people who were searching for effective measures to reduce the area of slavery and pension off the institution found their hands tied and their throats throttled. The South fought to preserve slavery by extending its territory: the answer to this was natural: and then, to muddle matters worse, the issue was mixed up with Centralism versus State's Rights. There were honest abolitionists who desired that the Union should break up into a Slave State and a Free State which would serve as a biblical city of refuge; there were slavery men who were reluctant to see the Union destroyed.

The smoke of warfare blinded the issue further. When it cleared away, the slave question had disappeared but the "Negro question" remained; and in the inevitable dictatorship of war, the central government, particularly the Executive, emerged, mystically raising aloft the Union as a mask for all its depredations. What the office-holders in the central government called "the menace of sectionalism," and what we may call equally "the promise of regionalism" was exterminated for fully two generations. Local life declined. The financial centers grew: through the mechanism of finance, New York and Chicago began to dominate the rest of the country. Presently the novel of "local color" appeared—proof enough that the color had washed out.

The Civil War cut a white gash through the history of the country; it dramatized in a stroke the changes that had begun to take place during the preceding twenty or thirty years. On one side lay the Golden Day, the period of an Elizabethan daring on the sea, of a well-balanced adjustment of farm and factory in the East, of a thriving regional culture, operating through the lecture-lyceum and the provincial college; an age in which the American mind had flourished and had begun to find itself. When the curtain rose on the post-bellum scene, this old America was for all practical purposes demolished: industrialism had entered overnight, had transformed the practices of agriculture, had encouraged a mad exploitation of mineral oil, natural gas, and coal, and had made the unscrupulous master of finance, fat with war-profits, the central figure of the situation. All the crude practices of British paleotechnic industry appeared on the new scene without relief or mitigation.

On both sides of the line many a fine lad had died in battle, and those who survived, in more subtle ways died, too. Some of them had evaded the opportunity for physical death: Mark Twain, after a brief anomalous period in the army, ran away to Nevada, William Dean Howells accepted a consular post in Venice, Stanley Hall, honest enough to record the point in his autobiography, accepted the services of a paid substitute. Happy the dead! The period after the war was the Gilded Age, with a vengeance. Sidney Lanier, who had served the South, and emerged a skeleton, faced the bitter truth of this great outburst of material enterprise:

The Golden Day

"Trade is trade but sings a lie:
'Tis only war grown miserly."

Unchecked, unmodified, industrialism controlled
the mind as well as the material apparatus of the
country: men who had a cut for scholarship, like
Charles Francis Adams, became railroad magnates,
and the son of the Great Emancipator became the
head of the Pullman Corporation. H. G. Eastman
founded the business school in 1855, and by the end
of the war that which was established in Poughkeep-
sie had more than a thousand pupils. The Massachusetts Institute of Technology was established in
1861 and dedicated to the practical application of
science in the arts, agriculture, manufacture and
commerce; when it was opened in 1865 the courses
on industrial technology dominated the whole program. The multiplication of these institutes witnessed the new orientation in industry and life.
"We do not properly live in these days," one of the
early Transcendentalists, J. S. Dwight, had written,
"but everywhere, with patent inventions and complex arrangements, are getting ready to live. The
end is lost in the means, life is smothered in appli-
ances." The Gilded Age accepted these facts with
complacence: business was the only activity it re-

spected; comfort was the only result it sought. Gone were the tragic doubts that had vexed the Transcendentalist and made life interesting and terrible and very beautiful for all the sensitive minds: the steel mill, the mine, the counting house, claimed them; or if not that, they went to an equally materialist post-war Germany, dominated by Bismarck and Krupp, and specialized in their *Fach*, as they might specialize in railroad securities or foreign markets.

One sees the great breach between the two generations in the biographies of fathers and children, in Henry James the elder and his two sons, or, more drastically, in Bronson Alcott and his far more famous daughter Louisa. Alcott, a son of a small Connecticut farmer, got an education peddling "notions" in the plantations of Virginia; and he became both a significant personality, and within the province of education, an interesting thinker: in an age that found Spencer too mystical and difficult, he was a walking embodiment of Plato and Plotinus. Louisa, one of his children, grew up in Bronson's household, worshiped Emerson, and looked upon her father as a well-meaning but silly old man. As a result, the daughter of the philosopher reverted on a lower level to the Yankee peddler: she became a hack writer, purveying lollypops and chocolate cordials to the middle-class market. Her realistic judgment and her bitter, merciless tongue were at the service of a childish fantasy: her fiction took the place in politer circles of the new ten-cent shocker.

Of all Louisa Alcott's books only one has survived for us. It is that which was made possible by the poor and abstemious life her father's silly ways had thrust upon his children in Concord. Little Women was the picture of a happy childhood: that was all: yet it contained so much of what every child had gone through, and so much of what a starved childhood would hope for, that it became universal. Louisa's imagination offered her nothing that she could pit against this memory: with all its scrimping and penury, the reality had been equal to the heart's desire. All America after the war turned to Little Women: and why? Was it not because the only meaning of their life had been in childhood? Maturity had nothing to offer them; it was only before they had started to make a living that they had lived. Boyhood meant home: maturity meant, not a larger home, but exile. Observe that the beam cast by Transcendentalism into the generation that followed was neither Nature nor the Duty of Civil

Disobedience nor the Orphic Sayings: no, Trancendentalism said nothing—except that childhood could be happy. That was a recollection that smarted!

Those who were born after 1850 scarcely knew what they were missing; but those who had reached their nonage a little before the great conflict knew it only too well. "How surprised," wrote one of them, "would some of those [Dial] writers be, if they should now in prosaic days read what they then wrote under the spell of that fine frenzy!" "We have found," wrote another, " 'realizing the ideal,' to be impracticable in proportion as the ideal is raised high. But 'idealizing the real,' as I shall maintain, is not only practicable but the main secret of the art of living. . . . There is a wise sentence in the otherwise trifling opera of the 'Grand Duchess' which says, 'If we can't get what we set our hearts on, we must set our hearts on what we can get.' " Excellent wordly wisdom! Doubtless it made one a little more comfortable as one tossed uneasily on one's bed at night, haunted by the ghost of what one might have been.

The post-war generation idealized the real, in its novels, which depicted so much of actual existence as might comfortably be exposed, and in its philosophy, which disclosed so much of the universe as could be assimilated to its feeble desires. As for those who knew better than this, what blighted figures they were—outcasts, almost beyond the pale of humanity, the sad, grim Melville, the proud macabre Bierce. They lived in houses that were dingy wells of darkness; and in the innermost rooms of these houses, cut off from the light in front and the light in the rear, their souls dwelt too, unused to either happy memories or good prospects. "Perhaps you know," wrote Lanier to Bayard Taylor, "that with us of the younger generation in the South since the war, pretty much the whole of life has been merely not dying." That held for the North as well. A good part of their life was merely not dying. Each of the principal literary figures of post-bellum America, Mark Twain, Ambrose Bierce, Henry James, William Dean Howells, William James, was the remains of a man. None was quite able to fill his own shape. They might doubt that a Golden Day had once dawned; but they had only to look around to discover the Gilt of their own. Well might the heroine of Henry Adams's Democracy say: "You grow six inches tall and then you stop. Why will not somebody grow to be a tree and cast a shadow?"

The Pragmatic Acquiescence

In America's Coming of Age, Mr. Van Wyck
Brooks first called attention to the broken rhythm of
American life, with its highbrows and lowbrows, its
Edwardses and Franklins, its transcendentalists and
empiricists. The gap between them widened after
the Civil War; for the war left behind a barbar-
ized population which had probably lost more civil
habits in four years than the pioneer had in the
course of forty. All that was left of Transcendentalism in the Gilded Age was what Howells showed
in the hero of A Hazard of New Fortunes—"an
inner elegance." The surviving idealist did not,
perhaps, particularly believe in the practical work
he found himself doing; but he did not believe in
anything else sufficiently to cease doing it. In a
quite simple and literal sense, he lacked the courage
of his convictions: what was even worse, perhaps,
was that he never acquired any new convictions that
might have given him courage. The post-war generation shows us nature-lovers like John Burroughs
but no Thoreaus, schoolmasters like Sanborn and
William Harris, but no Alcotts, novelists like Howells, but no Melvilles. It is not hard to define the

difference; to put it crudely, the guts of idealism were gone.

The mission of creative thought is to gather into it all the living sources of its day, all that is vital in the practical life, all that is intelligible in science, all that is relevant in the social heritage and, recasting these things into new forms and symbols, to react upon the blind drift of convention and habit and routine. Life flourishes only in this alternating rhythm of dream and deed: when one appears without the other, we can look forward to a shrinkage, a lapse, a devitalization. Idealism is a bad name for this mission; it is just as correct to call it realism; since it is part of the natural history of the human mind. What is valid in idealism is the belief in this process of re-molding, re-forming, re-creating, and so humanizing the rough chaos of existence. That belief had vanished: it no longer seemed a genuine possibility. As Moncure Conway had said: we must idealize the real. There was the work of a Howells, a Clemens, a James. It was an act of grand acquiescence. Transcendentalism, as Emerson caustically said, had resulted in a headache; but the pragmatism that followed it was a paralysis. This generation had lost the power of choice; it bowed to the inevitable; it swam with the tide; and it went as far as the tide would carry it. When Edward Bellamy came to express the utmost of its ambitions, in the utopia called Looking Backward, his mind dwelt lovingly on telephonic broadcasting, upon perfect public restaurants, and upon purchase by sample, as in the mail-order houses—all excellent devices, perhaps, but not in themselves sufficient to stir the mind out of its sluggish acceptance of the blind drift of things. One remembers that a little earlier than Bellamy a certain Danish bishop began to institute the coöperative commonwealth by reviving the folk-ballads of his countrymen.

III

William Dean Howells was, I think, the most pathetic figure in this post-war gallery; he so narrowly missed out. If only he had not been so full of the bourgeois proprieties, if only he had not been so conscious of the smug audience he was writing for; if only he had not looked so conscientiously for the smiling side of life, which he thought of as particularly American. Could any one read Melville or Hawthorne and think that this was the characteristic touch of the American imagination? Impossible. The smile that Howells tried to preserve, undimmed by tears, undistorted by passionate emotion, was only the inane mask of the booster. One is all the more moved to pity for Howells because, believing in Tolstoi, he did not really love the America whose sensibilities he so carefully protected: he appreciated its snobbery, its pettiness, and its cruelty towards its financial inferiors. But social good will was in Howells' scheme the principal, the standard virtue: he could not see that outright animosity might be preferable, if it led to beauties and excellences that mere good will neglected to achieve.

Howells' characters were all life-sized, medium, unheroic; he painted no heroes, because he did not see them in life. Alas! that was the best reason in the world for painting them. Life exists in the possible as well as in the actual: the must and the maybe are equally valid. The conscientious littleness of Howells was painful: a man who saw as much as he did should not lean on a gentlemanly walking stick. Mixing his love with prudence, Howells never went beyond the limits of conventional society: he could admire Tolstoi but he was incapable of his splendid and terrible folly. Howells had to a degree that should win for him forever the encomiums of our academic critics—the inner check. The inner elegance and the inner check were complementary parts of his own personality; and as a result, even the best of his novels, The Rise of Silas Lapham, never quite reaches the marrow; for these checks and these elegances were the marks of the spiritual castration which almost all his contemporaries had undergone.

Howells' failure, at bottom, was a refusal of the imagination, not of the intellect. His traveler from Altruria saw all the absurdities and hypocrisies and degradations of American life; but he saw them, as it were, only through a single organ, the eye; and in order to show their inadequacy, Howells was driven to comparing them with the practices of a quite mythical commonwealth. The point was not, however, that the American of the Gilded Age had fallen short of some imagined human excellence: the point was that he had not succeeded in establishing a merely human life. It was this perception that later enabled Mr. Sinclair Lewis to turn Howells' disgust for the contemporary scene into sharp satire, with an imaginative reality that is entirely lacking in A Traveller from Altruria and Through the Eye of The Needle. Mr. Howells kept his kindly feelings for Silas Lapham in one department; and his contempt for the abject and futile society the Laphams were creating in another; the result is that the fall of Silas Lapham was not a tragedy, since it was too petty and personal in scope, and the picture of capitalistic America was not an inescapable satire, just for lack of some such fully-fleshed figure as Babbitt to replace Howells' mannikins. Howells' imagination and his conscience did not work together: his figures all lack that imaginative distortion which takes place when a deep emotion or a strong feeling plays upon some actuality, like a blow-torch on metal, and enables the mind to twist the thing before it into a new shape. Babbitt is quite as human a figure as Silas Lapham; but he is actualized into something more than his apparent humanity by Mr. Lewis's contempt for the banalities of his existence. The fact that Howells' technical gifts were superior to Mr. Lewis's only heightens his essential failure as an artist, and enables us to see how tightly he hugged the limitations of the contemporary scene, and recorded them in his fiction.

In contrast to Howells' blind acceptance of middle class America, Mark Twain's rebellion, in the person of Huckleberry Finn, and his eventual pessimism, may seem to carry with them a more robust flavor of reality. But as a matter of fact, Mark Twain was caught as deeply in the net of the industrialist and the pioneer as any of his contemporaries; and if he gloried in being captured, he suffered, too, from its consequences. All that was durable in Mark Twain's work traced back directly to his boyhood and young manhood on the Mississippi before the Civil War: his life as a pilot had given him his one and only glimpse of the aristocratic man—the man who uniquely knows his business, as the old pilots knew the shoals of the Mississippi by the play of light or wind on the waters—the man who carries his point in the face of the crowd, as the Colonel defied the scurvy mob in Huckleberry Finn. In his mastery of pilotage, Mark Twain found himself; but he never sounded his own bottom so well in later life as he did in his career before the war. Mark Twain did not carry his sense of aristocracy to Europe with him; and when he refused to be "taken in" by the art galleries or cities of Europe, he was just as gullible in his refusal as were the new American millionaires, in their eager acceptance of bogus Rembrandts or Correggios.

Mark Twain's pessimism was as sentimental as Howells' optimism. Like his contempt for Europe, his contempt for mankind at large rested upon the unconscious cheapening of values which had resulted in the miserable struggle for existence that took place in a Missouri pioneer village, or a Nevada min-

ing camp. Mark Twain at first saved himself from
the impressions made by the blackguards and rowdies
he had been among in the Far West by taking as his
ideal their more civil counterparts, the industrialist
and the inventor: these types became his creators:
they alone were the people who furnished life with
an amplitude of meaning, and because of their works,
the Nineteenth Century was the "plainest and stur-
diest and infinitely greatest and worthiest of all the
centuries the world has seen." But at the bottom
of his soul, Mark Twain was revolted at the spectacle: he transferred his loathing of the current
brutalities to a Celtic twilight, whilst his memory
transformed the masculine smut of the roughneck
into the youthful self-conscious dirtiness of 1601.
He did not see that his Yankee mechanic was as
absurd as Arthur himself, and that for every folly
or vice or imbecility that may have existed in Europe, a hundred others were springing up in post-
bellum America. Mark Twain had an eye for the
wretchedness of the peasant's hovel: but apparently
he had never walked half a mile eastward from his
Fifth Avenue residence to contemplate the black
squalor of the new immigrant workers. No: for
Mark Twain industrialism was an end-in-itself; and

to fail to take it seriously and magniloquently was
to rob life of its chief felicities. As M. Regis Mi-
chaud has not unjustly said, in effect, comfort was
for Mark Twain the chief art of his period. Comfort put one in a mood to pardon anything that
might accompany the system which produced it!

Mark Twain's naïve worship of the paleotechnic
age was summed up in the classic, the marvelous, the
incredible letter he wrote to Walt Whitman in behalf
of a little committee of literary men on Walt's
seventieth birthday. It was written with an embar-
rassed avoidance of direct reference which makes
one wonder a little whether Mark Twain had ever
read Whitman; and it puts, better than any special
explanation, the perfect fatuity of the Gilded Age.
Here it is:

To Walt Whitman:

You have lived just the seventy years which are
greatest in the world's history and richest in benefit
and advancement to its peoples. These seventy years
have done much more to widen the interval between
man and the other animals than was accomplished
by any of the five centuries which preceded them.

What great births you have witnessed! The
steam press, the steamship, the steelship, the rail-

road, the perfect cotton gin, the telegraph, the
phonograph, photogravure, the electrotype, the
gaslight, the electric light, the sewing machine and
the amazing, infinitely varied and innumerable products of coal tar, those latest and strangest marvels
of a marvellous age. And you have seen even greater
births than these; for you have seen the application
of anesthesia to surgery-practice, whereby the ancient dominion of pain, which began with the first
created life, came to an end on this earth forever,
you have seen the slave set free, you have seen
monarchy banished from France and reduced in
England to a machine which makes an imposing
show of diligence and attention to business, but isn't
connected with the works. Yes, you have indeed
seen much—but tarry for a while, for the greatest
is yet to come. Wait thirty years, and *then* look
out over the earth! You shall see marvels upon
marvels added to those whose nativity you have witnessed; and conspicuous above them you shall see
their formidable Result—man at almost his full
stature at last!—and still growing, visibly growing
while you look. . . . Wait till you see that great
figure appear, and catch the far glint of the sun
upon his banner; then you may depart satisfied, as
knowing you have seen him for whom the earth was

made, and that he will proclaim that human wheat is more than human tares, and proceed to organize human values on that basis.

MARK TWAIN.

The thirty years duly passed: the marvels came —aeroplanes and dirigibles that assailed helpless cities; flame throwers and poison gases that suggested newer and more ingenious forms of torture than rack, wheel, or faggot; explosives and deadlier gases that threatened to exterminate not merely active combatants but every vestige of organic life in the region subjected to them. Towards the end of those thirty beautiful years, men applied, in a black rage of warfare, more satanic ingenuities than Mark Twain himself had dreamed of when he rigged up the defense which the Connecticut Yankee made against the feudal hordes in the last chapter, and slayed ten thousand men by a bolt of electric current. Man almost at his full stature at last! That the saturnine commentary on this letter should have come so punctually within the allotted generation is no doubt only an accident; but that Mark Twain should have dwelt on all these physical improvements, and never once have thought to mention that the Nineteenth Century was the century of Goethe,

Emerson, Tolstoi, and above all, of Whitman himself—that, I am afraid, was no accident, but the result of his fundamental barbarism. Poor Dante! Poor Shakespeare: thrice happy Whitman! Alas! of all the jokes Mark Twain ever labored to utter, this that fell so innocently from his pen was perhaps the wryest, and I am not sure but that it may cling longest to his memory.

IV

In a different fashion from Howells, Mark Twain was afraid of his imagination. Almost every time he felt an impulse towards poetry or beauty, he caught himself up short and mocked at it—and this mockery, this sudden passage from the sublime to the grotesque, became one of the stock ingredients of his humor. What did he sacrifice these fine impulses to? Nothing better than the accepted interests and habits of the utilitarian: he abruptly forgets the beauties of the Mississippi to tell the reader how many new factories have been started in Memphis, or he turns aside from the spectacle of the Hawaiian landscape to record the price of a canoe ride, or the difficulties of hiring a horse. Mark Twain's works were as full of scrappy information as an almanac: almost any externality interested him more than his own feelings, his own reactions, or the products of his imagination. In the experience of the mining community, the only uses of the imagination had been to tell tall lies: Mark Twain knew that use and employed it well in his many comic and admirable anecdotes: but he was not aware that the imagination might tell even taller truths, and at the faintest exhibition of this office, he would draw up quickly with a sudden grimace of embarrassment.

The futility of a society that denied, starved, frustrated its imaginative life, and had sacrificed every legitimate human desire for the spread of mechanical contrivances and the successes of finance, as Mark Twain himself was ready to sacrifice on occasion his most intimate convictions and do "not a bad thing, but not the *best* thing," in order to make himself more acceptable to his fellow-countrymen—this futility translated itself in Mark Twain's mind into the futility of mankind itself. In an established society, the solitary individual is always buoyed up in his weak moments by the traditions of his college, his profession, his family, his city: he feels the continuity of these institutions, knows that they have had good and happy moments; and looks forward to the time when they may come again. Pioneer society, having no past, and no continuity, could have no future, either. Men were corrupt: every man had his price: they were foolish: every one practiced his folly. Mark Twain had no notion that the pioneer settlement or the slick industrial town was a special and temporary phenomenon, something that had followed the breakdown of a great culture; and no more representative of a truly human society than the weeds that break into a garden which has fallen away from cultivation. The point is that human culture is a continuous process of choosing, selecting, nurturing, a process also of cutting down and exterminating those merely hardy and fecund weeds which have no value except their own rank life. "Choosing is creating, hear that, ye creating ones!" Thus spake Zarathustra.

Without persistently keeping to this process, human society tends to run wild, and in its feral state it serves no purpose whatever, and is empty, meaningless, unattractive. Cultivation is man's natural and proper condition; for life in the raw is empty. Like all his generation, Mark Twain was incapable of active choice. He accepted the values that surrounded him, and since they were not central human values—and he was too honest not to realize this—he stored up, secretly, the bile of despair. Man was an automaton: a mere creature of the forces that worked upon him. That he had also been a creator, and might be so once again—Mark Twain could not believe this. When he exercized his aristocratic capacities for standing alone, it was on minor and safe matters, like Christian Science and Foreign Missions. An automaton should not risk his mechanism on more precious human issues.

The depth of Mark Twain's despair was partly hidden by his humor; but in his contemporary, Ambrose Bierce, the mechanism of concealment was lacking, and all that one faced was the pitted earth, iridescent with the decay of dead bodies, like sullied black opals. Bierce's stories of the Civil War and his other tales of horror, were all filled with an honest and irredeemable blackness. He, too, had seen the very worst of mankind, on the battlefield and in the pioneer town; and all the horror of these grisly images remained with him, and colored his imaginative life. The potion Bierce brewed was too bitter for his contemporaries to swallow; and his work remained in relative obscurity, which perhaps only increased his sense of aloof contempt: Bierce's readers preferred a sentimental realist like Bret

Harte, whose local color was of the boughten kind. Bierce did not conceal his poisons: one drank them neat: and though they have an independent value as literature, in certain moods, one thinks of them here as an emblem of the dismal vacancy left in the mind by the devastation of the Civil War and the period of sordid peace that followed it. Bierce's qualities, unlike Poe's, were only partly temperamental: they arose out of an external experience which had no internal state to correspond with it outside the madhouse.

Warfare is in more than one sense a killing matter; and as the pioneer, on the testimony of John Hay, was usually old and gray before his time, so this generation of Clemens and Bierce, which had known both warfare and pioneering, and precious little of anything else, found themselves living in the shades of the charnel house. Thinking of the works and thoughts of these men, one wonders more and more what Howells meant when he said that the typical aspects of American life were the smiling ones. Was the pioneer happy? Was the returned soldier happy? Was the defeated idealist happy? And what of the industrialists who turned manufacturing into a form of warfare, surrounded their steel

works or pit-heads with barbed wire, and hired
armed thugs to defend their plants against strikers
—were they or their workmen in a smiling mood?
The open corruption of Grant's administration,
equaled only by that of the lamented administration
which followed the recent Great War, the graft of
Tweed rings and similar organizations in every large
city, the ugliness and filth of the growing industrial
towns—all these things formed a villainous pattern
for the mind to follow.

Men like Charles Eliot Norton, the friend of Rus-
kin, might be unhappy when they contemplated the
scene; but at least, they did not believe that the
Nineteenth was the greatest of centuries; and they
did not fancy that the followers of Watt and Smiles
were the highest types of humanity the earth had
known. But what of people who *did* believe in the
triumphs of the land-pioneer and the industry-
pioneer: what of those who thought these were the
Coming Men, and their works the final glory of
Progress? They might quote statistics till the
cows came home: they had only to look around them
to discover that, humanly speaking, they were in the
midst of a dirty mess. Machines got on: real estate
went up: inventions became more ingenious: money
multiplied: physical comforts increased: all these

achievements could not be denied. But men and women—they somehow did not reflect these great triumphs by an equivalent gain of beauty and wisdom. On the contrary, the nervous, irritable, scarred faces of Thomas Eakins' portraits cannot be placed alongside the strong, reposed heads, sound even if a little fatuous, that stretched between Copley and Morse; and beside the light that shone transparently in Emerson's eye, or the great sweet sanity of Whitman's body, or the wiry grace of Thoreau, the noblest figures of the Golden Age sagged and twitched a little. These children of industrialism were not the kind to keep cool and composed before a million universes: they lost their balance and their integrity before much less important things than a universe.

The Gilded Age tarnished quickly: culture could not flourish in that environment. Those who could not accept their external milieu fled abroad, like Henry James. As for those who remained, perhaps the most significant of all was William James. He gave this attitude of compromise and acquiescence a name: he called it pragmatism: and the name stands not merely for his own philosophy, but for something in which that philosophy was deeply if unconsciously entangled, the spirit of a whole age.

The Pragmatic Acquiescence

v

William James, born in 1842, became a philosopher by a long, circuitous route, which began with . chemistry, physiology, and medicine, and first flourished in its own right only as the century came to an end. As a youth, he debated over his capacities as an artist, and threw them aside. As a mature mind, he was ridden by an overwhelming interest in philosophy; but for twenty years or more he threw that aside, too. The deflection of his career from his innermost wishes was, one is inclined to think, the outcome of a neurotic conflict, which plagued him as a young man of twenty-eight. Equipped with a cosmopolitan education, and a wide variety of contacts in Europe, James returned to his own soil with the wan longing of an exile. Every time he greeted Europe, apparently, its charms increased his homesickness. He had for America some of the agitated enthusiasm and unguarded receptivity of a convert. He resisted Europe: he accepted America, and though he disliked at times the dusty, meeting-house air of Cambridge, he returned to it, and breathed it, as if it had descended from the mountain tops.

One searches James's pages in vain for a *Weltanschauung*: but one gets an excellent view of

America. He had the notion that pragmatism would effect an overturn in philosophy: but the fact was that it killed only what was already dead, the dry, unrelated rationalism of the theologists, or the vacant absolutism of idealists who chose to take the philosophy of Hegel without the concrete history which gave it a rational content. James's lack of a world view was due as much as anything, perhaps, to his positive dread of the difficulties of attaining one. In the crisis of his illness in 1870, under the influence of his newly attained belief in free-will, he wrote: "Not in maxims, not in Anschauungen, but in accumulated *acts* of thought lies salvation." Hence the fragmentary quality of James's philosophy. His supreme act of thought was his Psychology, a book over which he labored for a decade; but though the book is full of discreet wisdom and penetrating observation, carried to the limits of the scientific investigation of his day, James himself was dissatisfied with this act—it had impeded his progress towards Philosophy!

Beside the richness of Emerson's thought, which played over the whole field of existence, James was singularly jejune: he made up for his lack of comprehensive ideas by the brilliance and the whimsical reasonableness of his personality. He divested phi-

losophy of its high hat and its painful white collar,
and by the mere force of his presence made it human
again. His personality had the curious effect of
giving vitality to even moribund ideas; and the
superficial reader might easily mix up the full-
blooded James with the notions that lived again
through this temporary transfusion. He was above
all things the psychologist, commenting upon the
place of philosophy and religion in the individual
life, rather than the thinker, creating the philosophy
which should take the place. His pragmatism was
—was it not?—an attempt to cut through a personal dilemma and still preserve logical consistency:
he wished to retain some surviving representative of
the God of his fathers, without throwing over the
scientific method in the fields where it had proved
valuable. He used philosophy to seek peace, rather
than understanding, forgetful of the fact that if
peace is all one needs, ale can do more "than Milton
can, to justify God's ways to man." I am not sure
but that this search for anesthetics may prove in
the long run to be the clue to the Nineteenth Century, in all its depauperate phases. The use of ether
itself first came as a parlor sport in dull little
American communities that had no good wine to
bring a milder oblivion from their boredom; and

perhaps one may look upon anesthetics in all their physical and spiritual forms—ether, Christian Science, speed—as the culmination of the Protestant attack upon the senses. I throw this out by the way. The fact is that pragmatism *was* a blessed anesthetic.

If one could reconstruct New England in Emerson, one could, I think, recover great tracts of pioneer and industrial America from the pragmatists, the pioneer especially in James, the industrialist in his great pupil, Dewey. James's insistence upon the importance of novelty and freshness echoes on a philosophic plane the words of Mark Twain. "What is it that confers the noblest delight? . . . Discovery! To know that you are walking where no others have walked, that you are beholding what human eye has not seen before; that you are breathing virgin atmosphere. To give birth to an idea—to discover a great thought. . . . To find a new planet, to invent a new hinge, to find the way to make the lightning carry your message. To be the *first*— that is the idea." James's opposition to a block universe, his notion that salvation had to be worked out, his feeling that there was no savor, no excitement, no interest "in following the good path if we do not feel that evil is also possible and natural, nay, threatening and imminent"—what was all this, too, but the animus of the pioneer, translated into dialectic?

I do not say this to belittle James's interest in these notions: a philosophy must, plainly, grow out of an experience of life, and the feeling of boundless possibility that springs from James's pages was one of the healthy influences of the frontier. The point is, however, that a valuable philosophy must take into account a greater range of experiences than the dominating ones of a single generation; it is good to include these, but if it includes only these, it is still in a state of cultural adolescence. It is the remote and the missing that the philosopher must be ready to supply: the Spartan element in Plato's Republic was not familiar or genial to the Athenian temperament; but in the dry-rot of Athenian democracy it was the one element that might have restored it, and Plato went outside his familiar ground to take account of it and supply it. In Europe, James's influence has proved, I think, invigorating; for European philosophy had assimilated no such experiences as the frontier offered, and the pluralism and free-mindedness of James provided a release from a too cut-and-dried universe of discourse.

In America, however, James was only warming over again in philosophy the hash of everyday experience in the Gilded Age: he did not make a fresh combination, or a new application of these experiences; he was the reporter, rather than the creator. James's most important contribution to metaphysics was possibly his technical analysis of radical empiricism, which put relations and abstract qualities on the same plane as physical objects or the so-called external world: both were given in experience. But the totality of James's philosophy has to-day chiefly an illustrative value: woe to the seeker who tries to live by it, or find in it the key to a reasonable existence. The new ideas that James achieved were not so influential as those he accepted and rested upon; and the latter, pretty plainly, were the protestantism, the individualism, the scientific distrust of "values," which had come down in unbroken succession from Calvin and Luther, from Locke and Hobbes and Hume and Bentham and Mill.

James referred to pragmatism as "an alteration in the 'seat of authority' that reminds one of the protestant reformation. And as, to papal minds, protestanism has often seemed a mere mess of anarchy and confusion, such, no doubt, will pragmatism seem to ultra-rationalist minds in philosophy.

The Pragmatic Acquiescence

. . . But life wags on all the same, and compasses its ends, in protestant countries. I venture to think that philosophic protestantism will compass a not dissimilar prosperity." How curious was James's illusion that life was compassing its ends! That was just the point: that was what any one with a sense of history was forced to doubt when he contemplated the "prosperity" of Manchester, Essen, Glasgow, Lille, or Pittsburgh: life, distinctly, was not compassing its ends, and all the boasting and self-gratulation in the world could not hide the fact that something was wrong, not just in particulars, but with the whole scheme of existence. The particulars were all right in their place: men must delve and spin and weave and smelt and fetch and carry and build; but once these things get out of place, and, instead of ministering to life, limit all its functions, the ends for which life exists are not being compassed. The very words James used to recommend pragmatism should make us suspicious of its pretensions.

"For my part," cried William James, "I do not know what sweat and blood, what the tragedy of this life means except just this: if life is not a struggle in which by success, there is something gained on behalf of the universe, then it is no more than idle amusement." What is this universe which gains something by man's conflict? Is it not, perhaps, like the concept of "the country" which gains virtue by a boy scout's doing one good turn per day? The Hindu *guru*, the Platonic philosopher, aloof from this struggle, is not virtuous in James's sense; neither is the pure scientist, the Clerk-Maxwell, the Faraday, the Gibb, the Einstein—the activity of all these creatures, what is it but "idle amusement?" James's half-lost and half-redeemed universe satisfied the combative instincts: but life would still be amusing and significant were every vexatious devil banished, were every thorn plucked, were every mosquito exterminated! To find significance only in the fight, in the "action," was the signal of boredom: significant action is either the exercise of a natural function, or activity towards an end. It was the temper of James's mind, and it is the temper of protestantism generally, to take more pleasure in the obstacles than in the achievement. It has the courage to face danger and disaster: this is its great quality: but it has not the courage to face prosperity. In short, protestantism triumphs in a crisis; but it is tempted to prolong the crisis in order to perpetuate the triumph. A humane life does not demand this digging and dogging at the universe; it prospers as well in Eden as it does in the rorty wilderness outside. Growth, development, and reproduction are not categories of the battlefield.

With all the preoccupations fostered by the Gilded Age, which were handed down to the succeeding generation, it was inevitable, I think, that James's ideas should have been caricatured. His doctrine of the verification of judgment, as something involved in the continuous process of thinking, instead of a pre-existent correspondence between truth and reality, was distorted in controversy into a belief in the gospel of getting on. The carefully limited area he left to religious belief in The Will-to-Believe was transformed by ever-so-witty colleagues into the Will-to-make-believe. His conscious philosophy of pragmatism, which sought to ease one of the mighty, recurrent dilemmas of his personal life, was translated into a belief in the supremacy of cash-values and practical results; and the man who was perhaps one of the most cosmopolitan and cultivated minds of his generation was treated at times as if he were a provincial writer of newspaper platitudes, full of the gospel of smile.

The Golden Day

On the surface, these reactions betrayed little more than the ingrained bias of James's academic colleagues; and yet, as I say, the caricature was almost inevitable, and in his persistent use of financial metaphors he was himself not a little responsible for it. James's thought was permeated with the smell of the Gilded Age: one feels in it the compromises, the evasions, the desire for a comfortable resting place. Getting on was certainly never in James's mind, and cash values did not engross even his passing attention; but, given his milieu, they were what his words reënforced in the habits of the people who gave themselves over to his philosophy. Personally, he was "against all big organizations as such, national ones first and foremost; and against all big successes and big results;" but there was nothing in his philosophy that necessitated these beliefs in his followers.

An English friend of mine used to say that the old-fashioned London banker was often, like Lord Avebury, a financier and a cultivated man: the second generation usually remained good financiers, but had no interest in art or science; the third generation were complete duffers, and good for neither activity. Something like this happened with the pragmatists. There is an enormous distance between William James and the modern professors who become employees in advertising agencies, or bond salesmen, or publicity experts, without any sense of professional degradation; but the line that connects them is a fairly clear one. Of James one may say with sorrow that he built much worse than he knew. There was still in his personality a touch of an older and honester America—the America of Emerson and of Henry James, Senior, the America that had overthrown the old aristocracies so that every man might claim his place as an aristocrat. But the generation for whom James wrote lived in the dregs of the Gilded Age; and it was not these remoter flavors of personality that they enjoyed. As one comes to James to-day, one is touched by the spectacle of a fine personality, clipped and halted in its flight. As for his philosophy, one cannot doubt that it worked. What one doubts is whether the results of this work were valuable.

VI

It was those who stood outside the circle of the Gilded Age that have, within the last ten or fifteen years, come to seem more important than the dominating figures: Albert Pinkham Ryder in painting, Emily Dickinson in poetry, and Charles Pierce in philosophy. The overtones of the pioneering experience or the industrial scramble were absent for the most part in Pierce's writings; it was for that reason, quite as much as for their technical precision, that they remained unpopular. Pierce was not disrupted by the compromises and shifts of the Gilded Age: he lived his own life, and made none. As a philosopher, he thought deeply about logic, science, history, and the values that ennoble life; and his philosophy was what his own age deeply needed. It has remained for Professor Morris Cohen, in our own time, to resurrect his papers and to discover how fresh and appropriate they are, almost two generations after the first of them was published. Pierce had no part in the pragmatic acquiescence. His voice was a lonely protest. He was lost between two circles: the pragmatists, who were dominated, in Mr. Santayana's excellent phrase, by the foreground; and another group, equally pragmatic, equally a product of the Gilded Age, which was searching for a background. It is these latter who sought, in their own way, to fill up the vacancy that pragmatism left. William James belonged to one group; Henry James to the other; and the America after 1900 was largely the spiritual heir of one or another of these remarkable brothers.

CHAPTER FIVE

THE PILLAGE OF THE PAST

THE raffish vitality of the Gilded Age was not quite exhausted by manufacturing and gambling and astute corporate financiering. The pragmatists had indeed given depth to the adventure of industrialism; they had sanctioned the values that were uppermost; but they offered no clue as to what made a proper human life outside the mill of practical activity. The great captains of industry were caught within their own wheels, and were as helpless to escape as the meanest hunky who worked for them. One remembers Andrew Carnegie's resolution to resign from business in his early thirties, broaden his education, and settle down at Oxford or some other old center of culture: but the mighty wills that built the great fortunes were palsied as soon as they sought to withdraw from the game. In America, industry was not merely bread and butter; it was love, adventure, worship, art, and every sort of ideality; and to withdraw from industry was to become incapacitated for any further life.

Sooner or later, however, the reckoning was

bound to come. The position had been gained; the
money had been accumulated; the sons and daughters had come into leisure—well, what was to be done
with it? In the Gilded Age this question concerned
only a handful of people; but now that a vast ac-
cession of energies threatens the ancient economic
practices, based on manual labor and personal thrift,
with gradual obsolescence, the question has become
a universal one, since it begins to bear on a growing
army of workers, and not merely upon the minority
who have escaped work altogether. The answer
made by the Gilded Age is still the most popular
answer in America; and for that reason, it is perhaps not unworthy of scrutiny. The pragmatists
had tried to make a culture out of a partial and one-
sided experience; those who came into leisure and
money during the Gilded Age sought to achieve a
culture without any basis in experience.

Sometime during this period the epithet predatory millionaire was coined. It was strictly accurate as applied to the financial activities of a Daniel
Drew, a Rockefeller, a Carnegie, a Morgan; but it
was also appropriate in a wider sense. When the
time came to spend these accumulations, this generation turned out to have a predatory notion of

culture. Dissatisfied with the dingy environment of
Chicago, Pittsburgh, or New York, between 1870
and 1900, those who had the money and the special
animus began to look abroad for a cultural background. The merely practical men were still content to get their joy out of industrial enterprise and
financial manipulation in themselves; or they threw
themselves heartily into Civil Service Reform, clean-
ing up politics, the silver standard or prohibition or
trust regulation, or, with a daring sense of adventure, the initiative, the referendum and the recall.
The remnant who had lost active interest in these
things, continued to pursue them in sublimated
forms. Conscious of the emptiness of their lives,
outside the busy routine of trade, they sought to
fill up the tedium by spending money instead of earn-
ing it. What they had over from sport and fashion
went into art, and to the culture associated with its
ancient practices.

One might think that this attempt to acquire the
memorials of culture, on the part of a Mrs. Jack
Gardner or a J. Pierpont Morgan the elder, was just
the sporadic idiosyncrasy of the rich; but the same
movement was reflected in and incised into various
works of the mind: in the novels of Henry James,

in the historical memoirs of Henry Adams, and in
the great philosophic compendium by Mr. George
Santayana which rounded off and consummated all
the more genuine aspects of this effort. Where the
pioneer had gone west, the sons of the pioneer went
eastward; where the pioneer, looking upon Europe,
had been an honest boor, the new disciples of culture
had become a little servile and sheepish. At bottom,
this return to Europe and this absorption in the
externalities of art, architecture, and social custom
were part and parcel of the same movement: for they
arose out of an uneasy sense that the old culture
had gone, and a new one no longer filled the daily
life. The new pioneers in Europe were not the less
on the move because they were touring or sightsee-
ing; nor were they the less interested in pecuniary
goods; nor did their efforts, on the whole, produce
anything more than a sense of sublime sterility. But
there was this saving grace: the mind was a little
more active, and with all their several incapacities,
Henry James and Henry Adams and George Santayana were less subdued to banality than their
counterparts among the pragmatists: a good museum has after all something that a poor society
does not possess.

The Pillage of the Past

America may be defined by its possessions, or by the things that it lacks. On the second count our country is plainly a place without a long past, without a court and an aristocracy, without a stable tradition and definite connections, without the graces and souvenirs of an old and civil community. Those who feel that these deficiencies are intolerable now make what they can of the date of their ancestral arrival in the country, attempt to give the factitious aristocracy of riches the air of having long escaped from the factory or the counting house, and make up for the paucity of art in America by an exaggerated respect for the products of American craftsmanship. Sixty years ago, however, butterfly tables were still in the attic, and a good many of the "old families" had scarcely a grandfather to boast on the new soil.

The crudity and vacancy of the new American society had become apparent by the middle of the Nineteenth Century. Henry James has given his own testimony. "I saw my parents homesick, as I conceived, for the ancient order and distressed and inconvenienced by many of the more immediate features of the modern, as the modern pressed upon us, and since their theory of our better living was from an early time that we should renew the quest of the ancient on the very first possibility, I simply grew greater in the faith that somehow to manage that would constitute success in life." Henry James, Senior, was among the forerunners of the movement: the tide began to set definitely in this direction after 1870. Turning away from Nature, externalized and unassimilated, the new generation turned towards an equally foreign and externalized culture. The ugliness and sordidness of the contemporary urban scene could not be exaggerated; but they averted themselves from the scene itself, instead of confronting the forces that were producing it.

For the dominant generation of the seventies, the new personalities that had begun to humanize America did not exist: art and culture meant the past: it meant Europe: it meant over the seas and far away. Whitman was as remote as Dante: and did not Henry Adams himself, shrewdest if most pathetic of the children of light, not tell of his hopeless effort to come to terms with "Concord," and the reason, too? Henry Adams "perpetually fell back into the heresy that if anything universal was unreal, it was himself and not the appearances; it was the poet and not the banker." Well might he call this

heresy; for when the poet and philosopher no longer
feel at the bottom of their hearts that their world
is an essential part of that which surrounds them,
that it is that portion of the practical life which
has passed from necessity and routine into the domain of significance—when this conviction fails
them, they have indeed given up the ghost. A genuine culture was beginning again to struggle upward
in the seventies: a Pierce, a Shaler, a Marsh, a Gibb,
a Ryder, a Roebling, a Thomas Eakins, a Richardson, a Sullivan, an Adams, a La Farge were men
that any age might proudly exhibit and make use
of. But the procession of American civilization
divided and walked around these men. The pragmatists became more narrow, and lived more completely in their Seventeenth Century framework;
whilst those who espoused culture turned away from
the living plant, pushing through the hard, argilla-
ceous soil of the Gilded Age, in order to acquire and
hold the pressed flowers, the dead and dismembered
stalks, or the sweetish preserved fruits of Europe's
ancient cultures—authentic because they grew in
Europe, valuable, because they could not be produced in our own day, except by patent tricksters.

One does not know which was sadder, this pillage
of the past, or the condition which gave rise to it.

It began with an effort to be at home in Europe; the effort came into literature and took on form in the novels of Henry James. The American who loses himself in the Louvre, after having frittered away a gainful young manhood in commerce, and presently finds himself caught by a complicated and dense tissue of social custom—this figure might serve as a watermark for the general effort. James himself settled down in Europe and spent his whole life endeavoring to plumb this density. He sought to transfix in society what Whistler had so often tried to do in Nature—give a content to atmosphere and impalpability. He accepted Europe and its finish as the pioneer accepted Nature and its rawness: he did not want to do anything to it, he had no desire to assimilate it and make it over. Emerson, echoing the thoughts of every honest contemporary, had said that one could not become part of English society without wasting one's efforts in an attempt to transform it; he felt that identification would mean a loss of what was most precious in his own social heritage, and that struggle, for an outsider, would be quite futile.

Henry James, on the contrary, gave to Europe his entire loyalty; so far from wanting to change it, he wished rather to fix it: he could not be guilty of

republican satire, like Meredith; he could not lift
the scene to the level of tragedy, like Hardy; for
James to think obliquely of Sir Willoughby Pat-
terne's legs would have been to destroy the whole
illusion of culture in which, deliberately, he en-
meshed himself. Merely for an institution to be
"there" was to make it, for James, valuable. What
was interesting were the shades, the nice distinctions,
all the evidences of long-established usage. It was
not that James was altogether incapable of seeing the
shallowness and tawdriness of some of his fine people;
but for him these qualities were as nothing beside the
fineness, the fragility of sensation, which made them
so exquisitely what they were. Life might be many
things in Europe; but for the classes among whom
his imagination dwelt it was not raw. It had precisely what the American scene lacked: the implica-
tion of having been done a thousand times, until the
finest deviation from pattern became as violent as
a complete departure. Henry James treated in his
novels, in a remote gentlemanly way, the perplexities
and delights that the cartoonists in Life were touching in the eighties: he answered the question: "How
must one behave in Europe?"

It was useless to tell James that this acceptance
of Europe as complete, final, established, was only

an effort to wake the dead. What was alive in the Europe of James's day, the thought of a Tolstoi or a Nietzsche or a William Morris, had nothing to do with the Europe of place and precedent. That Europe was failing because its humanism had become dry and sterile, because what it called culture did not tend to become the shared possession of the whole community, because it was not steadily assimilating the results of commerce, science, and industry in new forms of culture, but was permitting these things to exist in the raw, and to slop over into provinces once adequately occupied by art and religion. James was no more conscious of the Europe of Nietzsche than he was of the America of Emerson: neither of these thinkers made any difference to him. As for the past, it was not a source of new life, but a final measure of what existed in the present. When one takes the past in this fashion, nothing new is good, because what is good is only what has been done before.

In short, Henry James treated Europe as a museum. By communing with its show-cases and its specimens, he could forget that the modern of Europe was precisely as inconvenient and distressing as the modern of his America. Europe's past was of course richer than America's—no thanks, however, to the forces that had been at work since the Seventeenth Century. Its valuable modern contributions were not limited to the old soil: the products of the factory and the laboratory were common to Western Civilization, and it was only in a mood of excessive self-abasement that the American need forget that from Franklin to Gibb, from Bartram to Cope, from Fulton to Edison, the American community had continued to produce figures which could stand easily on the same pedestal as the modern European. The medieval and renaissance past had left their rich memorials in Europe, and only vestiges in America; but in those aspects of life where Western culture had become poor and mean, Europe and America were both in the same state. What people had quickly come to call the Americanization of Europe—what was that but a falling away of the old garments of culture, and the exposure of the scraggly, embryonic form of a new culture, a skeleton without flesh, and without any central organ to control and direct its random motions?

If Europe had become more conscious of its physical plight under the new regime in industry, and had raised an Owen, a Carlyle, a Marx, to denounce the conventions under which the rich became richer and the poor poorer, in the new system as well as under the old, the American was equally conscious of the fact that the old culture had become impoverished, too, and that, though it had served well in its own day, it no longer sufficed. "The New Americans . . ." said Henry Adams, "must, whether they were fit or unfit, create a world of their own, a science, a society, a philosophy, a universe, where they had not yet created a road or even learned to dig their own iron." With the living effort to create such a new world, and so carry on the work of the Golden Day, the politer heirs of the Gilded Age had nothing to do. They did not merely bury themselves, with the aid of Baedeker, in the European past: they went a step further, they began to collect and embalm its scattered fragments, with a truly Egyptian reverence for the dead.

The Eighteenth Century had in its own phase of sterility converted the curio cabinet of the country house and the loot heap of the ruling dynasty into a public museum. These new and ardent disciples of culture went a step farther: they sought, not without success, to turn the contents of the museum back again into the private house. The leader of this movement, if one can single out one figure for this distinction among a whole host of successful and wistful and pushing people, was perhaps Mrs.

Jack Gardner, the builder of Fenway Court in Boston. She embodied the dream of her generation. She was in her time for "culture" what Mrs. Eddy was for "religion."

III

The dream of Mrs. Jack Gardner was fabricated slowly, according to her biographer, out of trips to Europe and a journey around the world. She was born in 1840; she thus escaped the crudities of the what-not period, when living rooms became mere albums of reminiscence, filled with picturesque memoranda in bric-a-brac. In 1873, Mrs. Gardner's biographer dutifully notes, she purchased "a small landscape," in 1875, a piece of stained glass in Nuremberg. In order to appreciate the importance of this departure, it is necessary to remember that John La Farge was beginning experiments with glass, and that Richardson was valiantly training a corps of stone-cutters, wood-carvers, painters, and sculptors during this period: after a spell of innocuous drabness, the arts were springing to life again in America: Eakins, Ryder, Blakelock, Fuller, and Homer Martin were all promising men. Mrs. Gardner was one of the first to take a decisive stand

[211]

against the threat of native art in America: she turned her face abroad, and invested all her interest and energy in works of art which were, culturally, securities—which had been on the market a long time, had reached par, and could be certified by trusty advisers, like the famous critic and appraiser, Mr. Bernard Berenson.

This hunting for pictures, statues, tapestries, clothes, pieces of furniture, for the epidermis and entrails of palaces and cottages and churches, satisfied the two capital impulses of the Gilded Age: it gave full play to the acquisitive instinct, and, with the possible rise and fall of prices in even time-established securities, it had not a little of the cruder excitement of gambling in the stock-market or in real-estate. At the same time, it satisfied a starved desire for beauty and raised the pursuer an estimable step or two in the social scale. It would be hard, in fact, to find a more perfect sublimation of the dominant impulses of the time than those which Mrs. Gardner gave vent to in her search for treasures; and of course, she was not alone: I have selected her merely as a representative figure, who did with some discretion and intelligence things that untutored Western millionaires did to their great grief—as well as the humiliation of their descendants—or that titans of finance, like Mr. J. P. Morgan, or Mr. Henry Frick did eventually on a masterly and exhaustive scale.

The essential character of all these culture-seekers was that their heart lay in one age, and their life in another. They were empty of the creative impulse themselves, and unwilling to nurture this impulse in the products of their own time. At best, they were connoisseurs, who could appreciate a good thing, if it were not too near: at worst, they were ragpickers and scavengers in the middens of earlier cultures. They wanted an outlet for their money: collection furnished it. They wanted beauty: they could appreciate it in the past, or in what was remote in space, the Orient or the Near East. They wanted, finally, to cover up the bleakness of their American heritage; and they did that, not by cultivating more intensively what they had, in fertile contact with present and past, but by looting from Europe the finished objects which they lacked. Their conception of culture, and their type of financial conquest, was already perfectly expressed in the museum. The Louvre and the British Museum, which have been the patterns of every other great collection, are the monuments of foreign conquest: they are the pantheons to which modern imperialisms bring back the gods and graven images of their subjects. It was the triumph of the American conquistadors to make the museum, filled with the scraps of other cultures, the repository of an irrelevant and abstract conception of culture for our own day —quite divorced from history and common experience.

For note this: the museum in America led inevitably to the baser sort of reproduction. There are two meanings to the word reproduction. One has to do with the results of bringing together two different individualities which mingle and give birth to a third, unlike either and yet akin to both. In contrast to this is mechanical reproduction, which takes a certain pattern, and repeats it a dozen, a hundred, a million times. *Cultures flourish in the first kind of living contact; and so far as the museum serves this end, it exists for a worthy and rational purpose.* When an exchange of traditions, however, results only in a mechanical reproduction, both the old culture and the new die together, for the finished products of an earlier age cannot take the place of something that must necessarily grow, change, modify itself, in constant intercourse with new desires and demands. It was in the second, mechanical sense that Mrs. Gardner and her cohorts

The Pillage of the Past

popularized culture in America. She seized scattered objects; lugged them to Boston; and enthroned them in a building which was—one hardly knows which to call it—a home and a museum. As a home, it became a pattern for the homes of rich people in America for a whole generation; and so, at tenth hand, it became a pattern for the poorest suburban villa, with its standardized reproductions of dressers and tables and carpets. Her home in Boston could, however, scarcely be called a domestic habitation; for one had only to open the doors and place a keeper at the entrance to convert it into a splendid museum.

That is what the Gilded Age called "culture;" and this is what they dreamed of. Mrs. Jack Gardner's palace was the Platonic pattern which earlier houses anticipated, and later ones struggled bravely towards. Was it any wonder that Henry James, William James, Charles Eliot Norton, Henry Adams sat more or less obediently at her feet? She had established in Boston an atmosphere, that elusive smell of aristocratic purpose for the sake of which Henry James had clung to Europe; she had brought together in Fenway Court the things Henry Adams respectfully, learnedly, quaintly pondered in Europe; she had created something which had not

existed in America before, something almost indis-
tinguishable from the original—an original becoming a little motheaten and down-at-the-elbows—and
she had done all this by the legitimated method of
her age, by magnificent strokes of bounce and bar-
gain. Was this not a happy compromise between
the spiritual heirs of William and Henry James?
The compromise sanctified business, because it could
buy "culture," and culture—that is, past culture—
was justified because it established a decent and
highly reputable terminus for business. When Mr.
Henry Ford restored the Wayside Inn, he was Mrs.
Jack Gardner's humble and deferential disciple.

Observing all this activity from a distance, one
can see that the transportation of objects of art
from palaces, churches, and houses in the Old World
to the homes and museums of the New was not, precisely, a creative act; but this fact does not seem
to have occurred to any one during the Gilded Age;
nor to have bothered any one if it did; and those
who still remain fixed in the pattern of the seventies
carry on this pious tradition without so much as a
quiver of doubt. The dead past remained dead: the
raw present remained raw: one was futile, the other
was overwhelming. That culture had ever been alive,
or that the human actuality had ever been more than

the brutal chaos which William James so frankly
accepted as the chief and undisputed ingredient of
existence—well, this no one could believe. How
completely these two poles of activity, the practical
and the ideal, were sundered one can see best of all,
perhaps, in the writings of Henry Adams. No one
in his time knew better the living reality of the past,
particularly of the Middle Ages in France, out of
which the museums looted their separate objects;
no one was more intelligently interested in the phenomena of his own day, the railroad, the corporation, the telegraph, the dynamo, the advances of
mechanics and physics. Yet no one, for all his
prophetic acumen, could have been more helplessly
immersed in the stream of events, and unable to
think himself out of them, than this quiet spectator.
With all his knowledge of the past, he too succumbed
to the pragmatic acquiescence.

IV

Henry Adams was a historian. Almost alone
among his American contemporaries, he responded
to Comte's great challenge; and sought to create
out of the mere annals and chronologies and fables
which had once been the stock-in-trade of the his-

torian, a more intelligible sequence, which would lead into the future as well as the past. This attempt to achieve scientific precision did not make him forfeit his imaginative penetration of the living moments of the past. His study of Mont St. Michel and Chartres which he began at a late period of his life, after having written about current events and the political character and fate of certain periods in American history was in many ways a model of historic reconstruction: he established the mood of his period, and built into the architecture and stained glasses of the churches he examined the theology of Aquinas, the science of Roger Bacon, the songs of the troubadours, and the simple willing faith of the common people.

Since Henry Adams saw so thoroughly into the Middle Ages with its cult of the Virgin, one might fancy that he would have seen with equal insight into his own day, and the cult of the Dynamo. He was, however, so deeply immersed in his own time that he unconsciously read back into history all its preoccupations and standards. When he came to forecast the movement of history in his own day, he immediately fell into the error of location. From the standpoint of mechanical inventions, it was plain that there had been a constant acceleration of movement since, say, the Thirteenth Century. This, however, was but one activity: had Adams projected himself back into the Seventeenth Century he would have been conscious, not of space annihilating machines, but the steady increase in the art of fortification; or had he chosen painting and sculpture instead of science and machinery, he would have noted the steady decline in their relative volume and importance. The rate of change had not necessarily increased or decreased; but the departments which exhibited change had altered. That Adams should have attempted to put all these complex historic transformations into a narrow physical formula dealing with the transformation of matter and energy, shows how completely his environment had stamped him.

William James knew better than Adams on this point; and when Adams published his essay on the Phase Rule as Applied to History, James pointed out that the current theories of science as to the eventual dissipation of energies in our universe had no real bearing on human history, since from the standpoint of life what mattered was what was done with these energies before they ran down—whether the chemicals make the pigment that go into a painting, or the picric acid that annihilates a com-

pany of men in warfare. Granted that the canvas
will eventually rot away, and the men will in good
time die: the only significant point is what has happened in the meanwhile. Qualitatively speaking, a
minute may hold as much as eternity; and for man
to have existed at all may be quite as important as
if he had an infinity of worlds to conquer, an infinity
of knowledge to understand, and an infinity of desires to express. A hearty, an intelligent, a believing age acts from day to day on the theory that it
may die to-morrow. In such periods of intensifica-
tion, as in Elizabethan England, the good may well
die young, because, with a complete life, death is not
a frustration. Adams, though he perhaps did not
realize it, was a victim of the theological notion of
eternity—the notion that our present life is significant or rational only if it can be prolonged. The
test of endurance is indeed an important element in
providing for the continuity of generations and the
stability of effort: it can be pragmatically justified:
but the notion that a quantitative existence in time
is a necessary measure of worth, without which life
is a blank, is a notion that occurs only when life is
a blank anyway.

Life, as Emerson said, is a matter of having good
days. Henry Adams was discouraged: his genera-

tion had had few good days. He looked forward to
the sink of energy at zero potential, or to the operation of the phase rule in history, as necessities which
canceled out the pang and penalty of human efforts.
If history moved inexorably from one phase to
another, in the way that a solid, under suitable conditions of temperature and pressure, became a liquid,
and then a gas, what mattered it that one was helpless—that one's generation was helpless? The in-
exorability of the law salved the laxity and the frustration. To picture a whole and healthy society,
Adams's mind ran inevitably back to the past! As
soon as he faced his own day, his mind jumped, as it
were, off the page; and beyond predicting a catas-
trophe in 1917, as Western Civilization passed from
a mechanical to an electrical phase, he saw nothing.
In accounting for the future, he was incapable of
putting desire and imagination, with their capacity
for creating form, symbol, myth, and ideal, on the
same level as intelligence. And intelligence itself left
only a dreary prospect! The products of human
culture outside science and technology became for him
little better than playthings. "A man who knew only
what accident had taught him in the Nineteenth
Century," he wrote, "could know next to nothing,
since science had got quite beyond his horizon, but

one could play with the toys of childhood, including Ming porcelain, salons of painting, operas and theaters, beaux arts and Gothic architecture, theology and anarchy, in any jumble of time."

There in a brief picture was Henry Adams's generation. Its major efforts produced the grand achievements of science and technology. Science, taken as a whole, was the highest product of the time; by successive extensions into fields unknown to Bacon or Newton or Descartes, by continuous acts of thought, by the application of the scientific procedure to the earth as a whole, in geology, to organic life, in biology, and to the human community, in sociology, science was breaking outside its Seventeenth Century shell and raising problems which the logical atomism of the older thought was incapable of even expressing, much less carrying further. As a world-view, the biology of the Darwinists was still too much tainted by Calvinist metaphysics; and the loose metaphors of mechanical progress, so patent to the observers of the Nineteenth Century, were too easily substituted as patterns for the life-histories of species and societies, whilst the mechanical technique of the laboratories, placed in the dull surroundings of the paleotechnic city, tended to put to one side problems which could be solved only in the field, or by carrying the environment of the field into the laboratory. The notions of organism, of organic environment, of organic filiation had still to claim a place beside the naïve externalities of the older physics. But with all its lack of philosophic integration, the acts of thought in Nineteenth Century science made all other acts seem fairly insignificant. Science was accepted as a complete organon of life; and all its provisionally useful descriptions became finalities.

Henry Adams was far from seeing that "the great and terrible 'physical world,' " as Geddes and Branford put it, "is just a mode of the environment of Life," and that desires and ends play as important a part in the dance of life as the matter-of-fact causal descriptions which alone he respected. The truth is, Henry Adams's generation had forfeited its desires, and it was at loose ends. It treated those objects of art which are the symbols of man's desires and masteries in earlier periods tenderly, wistfully, impotently. It loved its Correggios and Tintorettos; and its fingers lingered over velvets, brocades, and laces that happier peoples had worn; it rested in these old things, and knew that they were good. But the future had nothing to offer—except the knowledge that what is, is inevitable!

"The attempt of the American of 1900 to educate

the American of 2000 must be even blinder than that
of the Congressman of 1800, except so far as he
had learned his ignorance . . . the forces would
continue to educate and the mind would continue to
react." If that were all that there was to the social
process, one might well share Henry Adams's with-
ered Calvinism. For him, the only desirable future
lay in the past; what should have been a hope was a
memory. If the creative impulse were not, in fact,
self-renewing, if every generation did not, within its
limits, have a fresh start, if all the old objects of
art moldered away and nothing new ever took their
places—then Adams might well read only a dreary
lesson in the progress from Thirteenth Century
Unity to Twentieth Century Multiplicity. Europe's
spiritual capital was being spent; even those who
guarded it and hoarded it could not be sure that
what they called, for example, Catholicism was more
than a remnant of the spirit which had once integrated every aspect of life from the marriage bed to
the tomb. Steadily, Europe's fund of culture was
vanishing; and its fresh acquisitions were scattered,
insecure, far from covering every human activity.
The American could not live long even on his most
extravagant acquisitions of European culture.
William James was not another Aquinas, that was

plain; nor was Howells or James another Dante; and
the great figures Europe still produced, an Ibsen, a
Dostoyevsky, were far from getting complete sus-
tenance from their own day; they turned away from
it, rather, to folklore, philology, and the ancient
institutions of religion—the dream of a Messiah, a
new Christ or a newer Superman. Neither the
American nor the European had more than a bare
vestige of a faith or a plan of life.

> *Yet we have Gods, for even our strong nerve*
> *Falters before the Energy we own.*
> *Which shall be Master?   Which of us shall serve?*
> *Which wear the fetters?   Which shall bear*
> *the crown?*

Impotent to answer his own questions, Henry
Adams was still intelligent enough to ask them. But
he did not look for the answer in the only place
where it may be found: he looked for it in the stars,
in the annals of invention, in the credulous, mythic-
materialistic past.   He forgot to look for it in the
human mind, which had created these idola, as it had
created Moloch and Baal and Mammon; and which
might turn away from its creations, as the Israelites
turned away from the gods of the Philistines, once
their prophets gave them a glimpse of a more organic
and life-fulfilling world.

▼

The criticism and completion of these two phases of American development came in the first decade of the Twentieth Century. The instrument of this criticism, Mr. George Santayana, was born in Madrid and educated in Harvard and Berlin. He brought to the American scene and its characteristic vocations an aloof inquisitiveness: the very absence of the things in America which gave contour and significance to European society redoubled their hold upon the mind of this spiritual exile: one could almost describe what was absent in America by enumerating the ideas and cultural interests that found their way into his philosophy.

What was the nature of the sense of beauty? That was a question that William James never took up again in his philosophic writings once he had silenced the urge in his private life. What was the significance of the tragic poets? That, too, was an unseemly question in a country that read Lowell and John Muir. Finally, in the Life of Reason, Mr. Santayana broke away from the two main philosophic traditions of America, the highbrow and the lowbrow, the idealist and the empiricist, and returned to those richer pastures in which Plato,

Aristotle, and Lucretius had browsed. Far more successfully than William James, Mr. Santayana brought together the tender-minded and the tough-minded. He did this, not by declaring the existence of a province in which a decision must be made, not scientifically justifiable, but by giving a context to both science and idealism, or, to use the older terms, both physics and dialectics. If he dismissed idealism as an effort to re-create the whole world, and to seize upon the entire pageant as a product of mind —of man's mind (solipsism) or of God's mind (absolutism)—he restored idealism as a mode of thinking creatively, as the mode in which art and ritual take on an independent existence and create a new home for the spirit. Thus taken, idealism is not the will-to-believe but the will-to-create: it does not lead to a respite from practical activities but to a keener and intenser struggle, in a different medium. This struggle is not inimical to science; but it does not look upon the domain of science as the entire province of human thought.

Philosophically, the pillage of the past came to an end with its consummation in The Life of Reason. It has continued as a fact, and covered wider areas, but as an idea it could go no farther: that series of volumes was a perfect exhibition of culture:

it was in actuality what every other act of culture was only in vague intention—a recovery of the past, the whole past, particularly the remoter Ægean and Mediterranean past. William James said of the Life of Reason that it was grounded very deep, and would probably be looked upon as a classic by future generations: the fact that it has waited long for more than mere recognition shows the distance it went beyond the current prepossessions of the pragmatists and the culture-seekers. Mr. Santayana's thought was in a deep sense traditional; it was also, like every vital tradition, capable of bearing new fruits. In its justness of selection, its balance, its completeness, it was something that the Museums of the Gilded Age were quite unable to achieve within their own walls: it is still, however, a model of what they may reasonably aspire towards. Mr. Santayana's thoughts were not acquisitions but possessions; they were meant not merely to be exhibited but to be shared and absorbed.

In its richness of material, Mr. Santayana's philosophy had much in common with Emerson's; neither was content with an impoverished dialectic, and the academic philosophers, whose chief glory is to make bread out of straw, have frequently looked upon both thinkers as little better than amateurs and

[228]

dilettantes. But, unlike Emerson, Mr. Santayana had no roots in his own day and people; and this is perhaps the source of his weakness—his vanity and his preciousness. Such roots as he had grew out of the same Boston of the nineties which created Mrs. Jack Gardner's museum. Hence Mr. Santayana's resentful attitude towards the original and the contemporary: hence, too, his complete failure of intellectual sympathy, to say nothing of an occasional loss of urbanity, in dealing with a Browning, a Whitman, a Bergson. Catholicity is something more than an arranged gesture of the mind; it must grow out of a life that is itself complete. "Could a better system prevail in our lives," Mr. Santayana once wrote, "a better order would establish itself in our thinking." Lacking such a life, yet straining after it, it is no wonder Mr. Santayana's thought bears a taint of priggishness and artful effort: it was only, as it were, by a special exercise that he was able to preserve in the affairs of the mind an attitude so foreign to his milieu and his contemporaries.

If the Life of Reason does not impel us toward a new order in our own day, it nevertheless shows clearly what the great efforts of culture produced in the past. We cannot, indeed, make the ways of other cultures our ways; but by entering into all their life in the spirit, our ways will become more deeply humanized, and will, in fresh modes, continue the living past. When we are integrated, we grow like the tree: the solid trunk of the past, and the cambium layer where life and growth take place, are unified and necessary to each other. If the pragmatists had read this lesson from history, they would not have sunk entirely into the contemporary scene; and if the pillagers of the past had realized this truth, their efforts to establish a background would not have been so superficial.

CHAPTER SIX

THE SHADOW OF THE MUCK-RAKE

WITH the passing of the frontier in 1890, one special source of American experience dried up: the swell which between 1860 and 1890 had reached the Pacific Coast and had cast ashore its flotsam in a Mark Twain, a Bret Harte, a Muir, now retreated: the land-adventure was over. As a result, the interest in the industrial process itself intensified: the Edisons and Carnegies came to take the place in the popular imagination once occupied by Davy Crockett and Buffalo Bill. In books written for children there is a certain cultural lag which records the change of the previous generation very faithfully. The earliest children's books of the Nineteenth Century were moral tracts; they recorded the moment of Puritanism. The dime novel came in in the sixties, to echo the earliest exploits of the bad man and the outlaw; this was supplemented in the seventies by the books of Horatio Alger, written purely in the ideology of the Eighteenth Century, preaching self-help, thrift, success. In the late nineties a new set of children's books dealt with the frontiers and the

Indian fights of the previous generation, to be supplanted, finally, by stories in which mechanical experiment and exploit predominated. Here is a brief revelation of our dominant idola.

With the concentration on machine industry went a similar concentration in finance. The eighties and nineties were the decades of great improvements in the steel industry, in stockyards, and in the applications of electricity; they also witnessed the first rude experiments with the internal combustion engine, which paved the way for the automobile and the aeroplane. Unfortunately, finance did not lag behind technology; and the directors of finance found methods of disposing of the unearned increment derived from land, scientific knowledge, social organization, and the common technological processes, for the benefit of the absentee owner rather than for the common welfare of the community.

The note of the period was consolidation. The great captains of industry controlled the fabrication of profits with a military discipline: they waged campaigns against their competitors which needed only the actual instruments of warfare to equal that art in ruthlessness; they erected palisades around their works; they employed private condottieri to police their establishments; they planted spies among their workers; and they viewed, doubtless with satisfaction, the building of armories in the big cities where the State Militia could be housed in times of stress to preserve "law and order." Herbert Spencer looked to industry to supplant militarism; he had not reckoned that industry itself might be militarized, any more than he had seen that warfare might eventually be mechanized; but between 1890 and 1920 all these things came to pass. The workers themselves, after various efforts to achieve solidarity in a Socialist Party or in the Knights of Labor, met the challenge by adopting a pecuniary strategy: but unlike their financial antagonists, the captains of the American Federation of Labor permitted themselves to be handicapped by jurisdictional disputes and factional jealousies; and important new industries, like oil and steel, languished without even their modicum of financial protection.

What happened in industry happened likewise in all the instrumentalities of the intellectual life. This same period witnessed the vast mechanical accretion of Columbia University and Harvard, and the establishment of Leland Stanford (railroads) and the University of Chicago (oil). Stanley Hall recorded in his autobiography, with a noble restraint, the sort of ruthlessness with which President Harper of

Chicago made away with the corps of instructors and professors Hall had gathered together at Clark University: Mr. Rockefeller never got hold of oil wells and pipe lines with more adroit piracy. The concentration of publishing houses and magazines in New York was a natural accompaniment of the financial process.

This consolidation and concentration completed in industry what the Civil War had begun in politics. The result was a pretty complete regimentation of our American cities and regions. While the process was fostered in the name of Efficiency, the name refers only to the financial returns, and not to the industrial or social method. Without doubt large efficiencies were achieved in the manufacture of monopoly profits, through special privilege, corporate consolidation, and national advertising; but the apologists for this regime were driven to express all these triumphs in the sole terms in which they were intelligible—money. In spite of its wholesale concentration upon invention and manufacture, in spite of its sacrifice of every other species of activity to utilitarian enterprise, this society did not even fulfill its own boast: it did not produce a sufficient quantity of material goods. Judged purely by its own standards, industrialism had fallen short. The one

economist who devoted himself to explaining this
curious failure, Mr. Thorstein Veblen, was dismissed
as a mere satirist, because he showed that the actual
economies of machine industry were forfeited to pecuniary aggrandizement, and through a wry standard of consumption—which confused wealth with
pecuniary respectability and human vitality with
keeping up appearances. For the controllers of industry, financial imperialism produced considerable
profits; for the large part of the population it
resulted in a bare subsistence, made psychologically
tolerable by meretricious luxuries, once the sole
property of a higher pecuniary caste. The Pittsburgh Survey ably documented current industrialism in every civic aspect; but it merely set down
in cold print actualities which were open to any one
who would take the trouble to translate bank accounts and annual incomes into their concrete
equivalents.

It is no special cause for grief or wonder that the
Army Intelligence tests finally rated the product of
these depleted rural regions or of this standardized
education, this standardized factory regime, this
standardized daily routine as below the human norm
in intelligence: the wonder would rather have been if
any large part of the population had achieved a

full human development. The pioneer, at worst, had
only been a savage; but the new American had fallen
a whole abyss below this: he was becoming an automaton. Well might Mark Twain ask in despair,
What is Man? "I have seen the granite face of
Hawthorne," exclaimed Henry James, Senior, "and
feel what the new race may be!" In less than two
generations that feeling for a new human strength
and dignity had been wiped out. The popular hero
of the time was that caricature of humanity, a he-
man, shrill, vituperative, platitudinous, equivocating.
In art, the memorable figures, the human ones, were
caricatures: Mr. Dooley, Potash and Perlmutter,
Weber and Fields. They alone had a shape, a flavor.

The chief imaginative expression of this period
came from men who were caught in the maw of the
Middle West; and who, whatever their background,
had been fed with the spectacle of this callow yet
finished civilization, the last word in mechanical contrivance, scarcely the first faint babble in culture—
sentimental yet brutal, sweet but savage. F. P.
Dunne, George Ade, Ed Howe, Hamlin Garland,
Theodore Dreiser, Edgar Lee Masters, Frank Norris, Robert Herrick—these were the writers who
caught and expressed the spirit of this interreg-
num; and nearly all of these men had sprung out of

the Middle West, or had had at least a temporary
resting place in Chicago during their formative
years. Jack London and Upton Sinclair belonged
to this group in spirit, if not in locality. These
writers departed from the complacency of the Gilded
Age, if not from its pragmatic bias; they challenged
the esoteric culture that attempted to snuggle on
the ancient bosom of Europe in the name of a coarse
but upstanding vigor derived completely from the
life around them. Born between the close of the
Civil War and 1880, by the place of their birth they
had inherited the memories of the pioneer, by the
time of their birth, those of industrialism and the
new immigrant. Mawkish middle-class writers, like
Meredith Nicholson and Booth Tarkington saw this
life through the genuine lace curtains of respectable
parlors: but the more virile representatives of this
period knew it from the saloon to the stockyard,
from the darkest corner of the cellar to the top of
the new skyscrapers.

II

The shadow of the muck-rake fell over this period.
That was to its credit. But business went on as
usual and the muck remained. Those who defended

the sweating of labor, the building of slums, the
bribery of legislatures, the piratical conduct of
finance, the disorderly and short-sighted heaping up
of very evanescent material goods were inclined to
blame the muck-rake for the existence of the muck,
just as they would blame the existence of labor
agitators for the troubles they attempt to combat—
which is very much like blaming the physician for
the plague. As a result of the muck-rake, white-
wash cans and deodorizing solutions came into general use: philanthropic bequests became more numerous and more socialized; social work expanded from
the soup kitchens and down-and-out shelters to social settlements; and the more progressive factories
even began to equip themselves with gymnasiums,
lunchrooms, orchestras, and permanent nurses. If
modern industrial society had in fact been in the
blissful state its proponents always claimed, it would
be hard indeed to account for all these remedial
organizations; but in the widening of the concept of
"charity" the claims of the critics, from Owen to
Marx, were steadily being recognized.

Frank Norris, in The Octopus and The Pit, Upton Sinclair in The Jungle, and Jack London in the
numerous biographic projections he called novels,
faced the brutal industrialism of the period: they

documented its workings in the wheatfield, the prison, the stockyard, the stock exchange, and the vast purlieus of *la ville tentaculaire;* Mr. Robert Herrick, a little more restrained but just as keenly awakened, added to the picture. The work that these men accomplished could scarcely be called a spiritual catharsis; for it left the reader the same man that it found him; it was rather a regurgitation. To their credit, they confronted the life about them: they neither fled to Europe nor fancied that all American aspects were smiling ones. But these vast cities and vacant countrysides were not something that they took in and assimilated and worked over into a new pattern: it did not, in fact, occur to these writers that the imagination had an important part to play in the process. They were reporters, or, if they thought of themselves more pretentiously, social scientists; their novels were photographs, or at any rate campaign documents.

With unflinching honesty, these novelists dug into the more putrid parts of modern American society and brought to light corruption, debasement, bribery, greed, and foul aims. Fight corruption! Combat greed! Reform the system! Their conclusions, implicit or expressed, could all be put in some terse admonition. They took these symptoms of a deep social maladjustment to be the disease itself; they sought to reach them by prayer and exhortation, carried on by street corner evangelists, by legislative action—or, if necessary, by a revolutionary uprising in the fashion of 1789.

Perhaps the most typical writers of this period were implicated in political programs for reform and revolution. In their reaction against the vast welter of undirected forces about them, they sought to pave the way for political changes which would alter the balance of political power, drive out the "predatory interests," and extend to industry itself the republican system of government in which the nation had been conceived. Upton Sinclair's The Industrial Republic, which followed close on his great journalistic beat, The Jungle—the smell of tainted meat, which accompanied the United States Army to Cuba, still hung in the air—was typical of what was good and what was inadequate in these programs. To Mr. Sinclair, as to Edward Bellamy some twenty years earlier, the Social Commonwealth, full-panoplied, was just behind the horizon. He was hazardous enough to predict its arrival within a decade. With Mr. Sinclair's aim to establish a more rational industrial order, in which function would supplant privilege, in which trained intelligence would take the place of inheritance, in which the welfare of the whole community would be the prime end of every economic activity, I am in hearty sympathy. What was weak in Mr. Sinclair's program was the assumption that modern industrial society possessed all the materials essential to a good social order. On this assumption, all that was necessary was a change in power and control: the Social Commonwealth would simply diffuse and extend all the existing values. These writers accepted the trust, and wanted the principle of monopoly extended: they accepted the bloated city, and wanted its subways and tenements socialized, as well as its waterworks; there were even authoritarian socialists, like Daniel De Leon, who believed that the corporate organization of workers, instead of being given added responsibility as guilds, would disappear entirely from the scene with the Socialist State. Concealed under revolutionary phrases, these critics could envisage only a bourgeois order of society, in which every one would have the comforts and conveniences of the middle classes, without the suffering, toil, anxiety, and frustration known to the unskilled worker.

What was lacking in such views was a concrete image of perfection: the "scientific" socialists distrusted utopias, and so made a utopia of the existing order. In attack, in criticism, they did able work; but when it came to offering a genuine alternative, their picture became a negative one: industry without millionaires, cities without graft, art without luxury, love without sordid calculation. They were ready to upset every aspect of modern industrial society except the fragmentary culture which had brought it into existence.

Now, were the diffusion of existing values all that was required of a better social order, the answer of capitalism was canny and logical: the existing regime could diffuse values, too. Did not bank accounts spread—and Ford cars—and movies—and higher wages in the skilled trades? What more could one want? Why risk one's neck for a Social Commonwealth when, as long as privilege was given a free hand, it would eventually provide the same things? Thus the socialist acceptance of the current order as a "necessary stage," and the socialist criticism, "Capitalism does not go far enough" have been answered by the proposition that it actually does go farther: the poor do not on the whole get poorer, but slowly march upward in the social scale.

The evils of privilege and irresponsible power in America were of course real; but the essential poverty of America was a qualitative poverty, one which cut through the divisions of rich and poor; and it has been this sort of poverty which has prevented us from projecting in the imagination a more excellent society. Life was more complicated in America but not more significant; life was richer in material goods but not in creative energies. These eager and relentless journalists were unaware of the necessity for establishing different kinds of goods than the existing ones; they had no notion of other values, other modes, other forms of activity than those practiced by the society around them. The result is that their works did not tend to lead out of the muddle. Their novels were interesting as social history; but they did not have any formative effect: for they sentimentalized the worker to the extent of always treating him as a victim, and never making out of him a hero. The only attempt to create a heroic portrait of the worker came towards the end of the muck-raking period; it was that of Beaut McGregor in Sherwood Anderson's Marching Men, a half-wrought figure in an imperfect book.

What the American worker needed in literature was discipline, confidence, heroic pictures, and large aims: what he got even from the writers who preached

his emancipation was the notion that his distressing
state was only the result of the capitalist's villainy
and his own virtues, that the mysterious external
forces of social evolution were bound eventually to
lift him out of his mean and subservient condition
and therefore he need not specially prepare himself
to bring about this outcome—and that anyway the
odds were always against him! It is doubtful
whether this analysis could be called accurate
science; it certainly was not high literature. For
all the effect that these painstaking pictures had
in lifting the worker onto a more active plane of
manhood, one would willingly trade the whole literature for a handful of good songs. I am not sure
but that the rowdy, impoverished lyrics of the wob-
blies were not more stirring and formative—and that
they may last longer, too.

III

There were two writers who stood outside this
gallery: Jack London, who created his own Superman, and Mr. Theodore Dreiser, who depicted the
whole American scene without any propagandist bias.
They do not alter the contours of the picture; they
merely show how futile the will-to-power and the

desire to face facts became, when pushed to their conclusions without reference to rational ends.

Jack London came to maturity in the nineties; and after a career as oyster pirate in San Francisco Bay, as a tramp with Coxey's army, as an adventurer in Alaska, after participating in all the coarse and wearing manual labor that may offer itself to a willing lad, he acquired the scraps of an education, and went in for writing, as an easier kind of livelihood. He quickly achieved popularity. He had only to tell his life over again—to make a story of it in the newspaper sense—to feed the romanticism of the big urban populations which now began to swallow the five, ten, and fifteen cent magazines. London became a sort of traveling salesman of literature, writing to his market, offering "red blood" and adventure to people who were confined to ledgers, ticker-tapes, and Sunday picnics. He brandished the epithet socialist as a description of himself and his ideas; but he was gullible enough to swallow Kipling's doctrine of the White Man's Burden, believed in the supremacy of the Nordics, who were then quaintly called Anglo-Saxons, and clung to socialism, it would seem, chiefly to give an additional luster of braggadocio and romanticism to his career; for socialism, to London's middle-class contemporaries, was an adventure more desperate than the rush for gold in the Klondike. Superficially London perhaps believed in the socialist cause; but his personal activities had scarcely the chemical trace of a public interest in them; and one need only go below the surface to see that he betrayed his socialism in all his ingrained beliefs, particularly, his belief in success, and in his conception of the Superman.

The career of the Superman in America is an instructive spectacle. He sprang, this overman, out of the pages of Emerson; it was Emerson's way of expressing the inexhaustible evolutionary possibilities of a whole race of Platos, Michelangelos, and Montaignes. Caught up by Nietzsche, and colored by the dark natural theology Darwin had inherited from Malthus, the Superman became the highest possibility of natural selection: he served as a symbol of contrast with the coöperative or "slave morality" of Christianity. The point to notice is that in both Emerson and Nietzsche the Superman is a higher type: the mark of his genius is the completer development of his human capacities. London, like his whole generation, scarcely knew of Emerson's existence: one has only to note the way in which Frank Norris respectfully refers to "great"

The Shadow of the Muck-rake

New England writers like Lowell and Whittier to
know that he had probably not read even these minor
writers. London, however, seized the suggestion of
the Superman and attempted to turn it into a
reality. And what did he become? Nothing less
than a preposterous bully, like Larssen, the Sea-
Wolf, like Burning Daylight, the miner and adventurer, like his whole gallery of brutal and brawny
men—creatures blessed with nothing more than the
gift of a magnificent animality, and the absence of a
social code which would prevent them from inflicting
this gift upon their neighbors. In short, London's
Superman was little more than the infantile dream
of the messenger boy or the barroom tough or the
nice, respectable clerk whose muscles will never quite
stand up under strain. He was the social platitude
of the old West, translated into a literary epigram.

What London called "white logic," which he
sought to erase by drink, was the perception that
life, as he had found it, was empty. The logic was
faultless; the insight was just; but as a writer and
a mythmaker it remained for him to fill it up, to
use the materials he had gathered as the painter
uses his pigments, to create a more significant pattern. To do this he was impotent: hence his "scientific" determinism. "You made me what I am

to-day: I hope you're satisfied." This, in the words
of a popular ballad, was the retort of the handicapped and limited American artist to his environment. He held a mirror up to society; and to read
the mind of a London or a Dreiser is to read what
was passing in the streets about him; or, vice-versa,
to record as in a lens the dull parade of men, women,
factories, downtowns, waterfronts, suburbs, railroads, murders, lusts, connubialities, successes, chi-
canes, is to read their novels.

The bewildered chaos of the sons of the pioneer,
as they reached their destination and recoiled into
muzzy reflection, is best illustrated, I think, in the
novels of Mr. Theodore Dreiser. Mr. Dreiser has
a power and reach which set him well above his
immediate contemporaries. Across the panorama
of the mid-American prairie, where Chicago sits like
the proverbial spider in the midst of her steel web,
Mr. Dreiser flung his canvas; his Philadelphia, too,
is spiritually part of that Chicago. Huge figures,
titans of finance, who practice "art for art's sake"
in the pursuit of money, or "geniuses" in art, who
are business men in everything except their medium,
dominate the scene; they wander about, these
Cowperwoods and Witlas, like dinosaurs in the ooze
of industrialism. Mr. Dreiser's books reflect this

bulk and multitudinousness: they are as full of
details as a day's shopping: with a vast hippo-
potamus yawn he swallowed the minutiæ of America's physical activities: you might find in his books
the wages of laundry wagon drivers in 1894, the
style of women's gloves in 1902, how one cashes a
check at a bank, the interior arrangements of a
modern hotel, the details of a criminal prosecution.

By what means does he handle this material?
What makes it significant? There are no means; or
rather, they are those of the census taker, whose
schedule covers everything. There is a superficial
resemblance between Dreiser and Zola; but Zola,
being the product of the old and high civilization
of Provence, had some conception of what a humane
life might be, and not for a second was he unconscious of his purpose to criticize the church, to
portray the evils of drunkenness, to expose the
brutalities of the farm or the steel works: he had the
advantage of describing a society that had known
better days, and these days were his implicit point
of reference. What can we say of Mr. Dreiser? He
is simply bewildered. He is attracted to anything
that exhibits size, power, sexual lust; believing in
these things alone, he is critical of any institution
or idea that stands in their way. His heroes know

what it is to have material success and to conquer
women; but their conquests lead nowhere and develop into nothing. One thing bobs up; another falls
down; and in the long run none of their affairs,
financial or sexual, are of any consequence. It is
a picture of society: yes: but so is the Sunday newspaper.

One wonders about the curious naïveté of Mr.
Dreiser's mind. He is free from conventional restraints; he has the healthy indifference of the honest physician who encounters everything in the day's
work. He thinks other people ought to be free, too;
and he can scarcely see that there are any consequences in sexual passion, for example, except a
conflict with the formalities of the social code. The
reaction of the wife of the "Genius" to his adventures with other women seem to the hero irrelevant;
they are due, not to the inherent psychology of the
relationship, but to her being conventionally brought
up! In his callowness, in his heavy platitudes, in
his superficial revolt against "morality," Mr.
Dreiser was but the forerunner of a host of magazines that live on "confessions," fabricated or real,
of ordinary men and women, without any more sense
of direction or purpose or humane standards than
Mr. Dreiser's own heroes and heroines. His novels

are human documents; so is a pair of shoestrings, a torn glove, a footprint. But the chief thing they give evidence of is the total evaporation of values in the modern industrial environment, the feebleness of the protestant morality, which was all that kept the social bond from breaking entirely in the old days; and the total lack, in this crass new life, of any meanings or relationships beyond the raw fact.

Culture in its many ramifications is a working over of the raw fact. Just as eating, among civilized peoples, is not a mere hacking and gnawing at flesh and bones, but an occasion for sociability and civil ceremonies, to the extent that the ceremony frequently becomes as important as the fact itself and works out into a separate drama, so every act tends to be done, not just for its own sake, but for the social values that accompany it: the taste, the conversation, the wit, the sociability are esthetic filaments that bind men together and make life more pleasing. To the extent that these shared meanings come into existence and spread over all the details of the day's activities, a community is cultured; to the extent that they disappear, or have no place, it is barbarous. The hurried business man who snatches his lunch, snatches his girl in the same way: his lust is as quickly exhausted as his appetite; and

he looks around for a new stimulus, as he might
scan the menu for a new dish. Experience of this
sort tends to be truncated; it remains on the level
of the physical fact, and the physical fact becomes
dull and unimportant, and must be succeeded by new
stimuli, which eventually become stale, too. Culture,
on the other hand, implies the possibilities of repeti-
tion. Like fine poetry or music, the hundredth occasion often finds an act as interesting as the first.
If this were not so, life would be intolerable; and
because it is so, it is no wonder that the barbarians
Mr. Dreiser portrays find all their adventures stale,
and all their different achievements tending towards
a deadly sameness. Their lives are empty, because
lust and power are empty, so long as they do not
contrive situations in which power is turned to rational ends and produces efficient industries, fine
cities, and happy communities—or sexual passion
its friendship, its salon, its home, its theater in
which the private interest becomes sublimated and
amplified into more agreeable forms of social life.

IV

Among the group of New Englanders established
in Chicago at the beginning of the century, Mr.

John Dewey was perhaps the most distinguished. Among all the writers of this milieu and period, he expressed in his philosophy something more than the mere welter of existence. From the beginning Mr. Dewey was bracketed with William James as one of the founders and developers of pragmatism, or as he himself preferred to call it, instrumentalism; but, in spite of similarities of approach, there were differences between these men which at bottom reflected the intervening of almost a generation between the birth of James and that of Dewey.

William James had a style. Dreiser, Dewey, the commanding writers of the early Chicago school, were at one on this point: they had no style: they wrote in a language which, however concrete its objects, was as fuzzy and formless as lint. There is a homely elegance in James's writing, a beauty in the presentation of the thought, even if the concept of beauty was absent from his philosophy; in the earlier writing of Dewey, on the other hand, one looks in vain for either the concept or its literary equivalent. The comedown is serious. Style is the indication of a happy mental rhythm, as a firm grip and a red cheek are of health. Lack of style is a lack of organic connection: Dreiser's pages are as formless as a dumpheap: Mr. Dewey's pages are as depressing as a subway ride—they take one to one's destination, but a little the worse for wear. Mr. Randolph Bourne once characterized this quality of Mr. Dewey's mind as "protective coloration;" and the phrase is accurate enough if one means that the creature has identified himself in shape and color with his environment. No one has plumbed the bottom of Mr. Dewey's philosophy who does not feel in back of it the shapelessness, the faith in the current go of things, and the general utilitarian idealism of Chicago—the spirit which produced the best of the early skyscrapers, the Chicago exposition, Burnham's grandiose city plan, the great park and playground system, the clotted disorder of interminable slums, and the vitality of a handful of experimental schools.

Mr. Dewey's philosophy represents what is still positive and purposeful in that limited circle of ideas in which the American mind was originally born; he is at home in the atmosphere of protestantism, with its emphasis upon the rôle of intelligence in morals; in science, with its emphasis upon procedure, technique, and deliberate experiment; and he embraces technology with the same esthetic faith that Mr. Henry Ford embraces it. Above all, Mr. Dewey believes in democracy; that was at the bottom of his

many acceptances of the milieu; what had been produced by the mass of men must somehow be right,
and must somehow be more significant than the
interests which occupy only a minority! In Mr.
Dewey the American mind completed, as it were, its
circle, and returned to its origin, amplifying, by
the experience of a century, the essential interests of
an Edwards, a Franklin, a Paine.

To the things that stand outside this circle of
ideas, Mr. Dewey has been essentially antagonistic,
or at least unsympathetic. He has been a severe
and just critic of conventional education; and he
has undermined conceptions of philosophy, art, and
religion which represented merely the mummified
experiences and aims of other generations: but his
criticisms have been conducted with an unqualified
belief in the procedures of common sense and technology, because these procedures have led to practical "results." Happiness, too, for him "is found
only in success; but success means succeeding, getting
forward, moving in advance. It is an active process,
not a passive outcome." That is quite another definition of happiness than the equilibrium, the point
of inner rest, which the mystic seeks; but for Mr.
Dewey a less active and utilitarian kind of happiness always tends to be "totally separated from re-

newal of the spirit." In other words, happiness means for Mr. Dewey what it meant for the pioneer: a preparation for something else. He scarcely can conceive that activity may follow the mode of the circle or the pendulum, rather than the railroad train.

In spite of all these opacities, it would be absurd to ignore the great service that instrumentalism has performed; for it has crystallized in philosophic form one of the great bequests of science and modern technology: the respect for coöperative thinking and for manual activity—experiment and invention—in guiding and controlling this process. The notion that action by itself was undignified and foreign to the life of the mind was, of course, a leisure class superstition. Creative thought is not a polite shuffling of observations, memories, and *a priori* logic: that is but one phase of the whole process: man thinking is not a spectatorial "mind" but a completely operative human organism, using in various degrees and at various stages every part of his organism, down to his viscera, and every available form of tool, from the finger which might trace a geometrical theorem in the sand to the logarithm table or the electric furnace. The otiose, leisure-class notion of thinking is that it is the reflection of what one reads in a book or gets by hearsay from other people: the great achievement of the scientific method was to supplant the scholar's chair—which does in fact peculiarly serve one phase of the thinking-process—by the work of the field and the laboratory, by exploration, observation, mechanical contrivance, exact measurement, and coöperative intercourse. With the introduction of the scientific method, men began to think consciously as whole human beings: the worker, the rambler, the traveler, the explorer, enlarged the scope of the mind. If this movement was accompanied by some loss, perhaps, in that part of the thinking process covered by dialectics, the gain was nevertheless a great one.

Mr. Dewey seized upon this achievement and brought out its significance admirably. Its implications should not be neglected. According to Dewey, thought is not mature until it has passed into action: the falsity of philosophy is that it has frequently dealt with ideas which have no such issue, while the weakness of the practical world is that its actions are unintelligent routine, the issue of an unreflective procedure. Action is not opposed to ideas: the means are not one thing, and the final result of attending to them quite another: they are not kitchen maids and parlor guests, connected only by being in the same house. Means which do not lead to significant issues are illiberal and brutal; issues which do not take account of the means necessary to fulfill them are empty and merely "well-meaning." A transcendentalism which takes such high ground poor humanity cannot stand on it, or an empiricism which takes such low ground that it introduces no excellence into brute existence—both these things are inimical to life, and absurd—and it has been Mr. Dewey's great merit to point out this absurdity, and so open the way to a more complete kind of activity, in which facts and values, actualities and desires, achieve an active and organic unity.

In its flexibility, in its experimentalism, in its emphasis upon the ineptitude of any finality, except that involved in the process of living itself, with the perpetual intercourse between the organism and its implicated environment, Mr. Dewey's philosophy expresses a continuously formative part of our American experience. For the European, roughly speaking, history is what prevents anything new or fresh from being done. It needed the dislocation of settling a New World to discover a to-morrow not actually given in a host of yesterdays. In so far as Mr. Dewey has given expression to these things, his work has been to the good: it is not that flexibility and experiment are good in themselves: there are times when it is necessary to be as stiff as a ramrod and as dogmatic as a Scotch dominie—but these things represent a genuine addition to the European experience of life, and to introduce them as categories in philosophy is to extend its boundaries.

The deficiencies of Mr. Dewey's philosophy are the deficiencies of the American scene itself: they arise out of his too easy acceptance of the Seventeenth and Eighteenth Century framework of ideas; and although he has written about the influence of Darwinism on philosophy, and has done some of his best work in enriching the concepts of philosophy with biological illustrations and clues, he has not been sufficiently critical of the doctrines and writers whose works lean closest to his own habits of thinking. The utilitarian type of personality has been for the instrumentalist a thoroughly agreeable one: I recollect eulogies of Bacon in Mr. Dewey's works, but none of Shakespeare; appreciations of Locke, but not of Milton; of Bentham, but not Shelley and Keats and Wordsworth and Blake. The thinkers who saw social welfare as the principal object of existence, and who naïvely defined it in terms of man's control over the externalities of his environment, through the employment of science and technology, have been nearest to Mr. Dewey's heart. He has even written as if the telephone did away with the necessity for imaginative reverie—as if the imagination itself were just a weak and ineffectual substitute for the more tangible results of invention!

This aspect of Mr. Dewey's instrumentalism is bound up with a certain democratic indiscriminateness in his personal standards: a Goodyear and a Morse seem to him as high in the scale of human development as a Whitman and a Tolstoi: a rubber raincoat is perhaps a finer contribution to human life than "Wind, Rain, Speed." What indeed is his justification for art? Let him answer in his own words. "Fine art, consciously undertaken as such, is peculiarly instrumental in quality. It is a device in experimentation, carried on for the sake of education. It exists for the sake of a specialized use, use being a training of new modes of perception. The creators of such works are entitled, when successful, to the gratitude that we give to inventors of microscopes and microphones; in the end they open new objects to be observed and enjoyed." This is a fairly back-handed eulogy, unless one remembers Mr. Dewey's intense gratitude for all mechanical instruments.

In a similar mood, Mr. Dewey speaks of the

"intrinsic worth of invention;" but the point is, of course, that except for the inventor, who is *ipso facto* an artist, the invention is good for what it leads to, whereas a scene in nature, a picture, a poem, a dance, a beautiful conception of the universe, are good for what they are. A well-designed machine may also have the same kind of esthetic value: but the independent joy it gives to the keen mechanic or engineer is not the purpose of its design: whereas art has no other purpose; and when a Duchamps-Villon or a Man Ray wants to create the esthetic equivalent of a machine, he does not employ an engineer, but goes through the same process he would undergo to model the figure of a man. Esthetic enjoyment will often lead to other things, and it is all the happier for doing this: the scene in nature may lead to the planting of a park, the dance may promote physical health: but the essential criterion of art is that it is good without these specific instrumental results, good as a *mode of life*, good as a beatitude. An intelligent life, without these beatitudes, would still be a poor one: the fact that Bentham could mention pushpins in the same breath as poetry shows the deeply anesthetic and life-denying quality of the utilitarian philosophy.

There are times when Mr. Dewey seems ready to admit this deficiency. In Reconstruction in Philosophy he was aware of the danger of utilitarian monsters, driving hard bargains with nature, and he was appreciative, to a degree unusual in his thought, of the contemplative life, with its loving intercourse with forms and shapes and symbols in their immediacy. The weakness of Mr. Dewey's instrumentalism is a weakness of practical emphasis. He recognizes the place of the humane arts, but his preoccupation has been with science and technology, with instrumentalism in the narrow sense, the sense in which it occurs to Mr. Babbitt and to all his followers who practice so assiduously the mechanical ritual of American life. Conscious of the weakness of the academic critic, who may take art as an abstract end-in-itself, quite divorced from life and experience, he forgets that Mr. Babbitt treats showerbath fixtures and automobile gadgets in the same way—as if a life spent in the pursuit of these contrivances was a noble and liberal one. What Mr. Dewey has done in part has been to bolster up and confirm by philosophic statement tendencies which are already strong and well-established in American life, whereas he has been apathetic or diffident about things which must still be introduced into our scheme of things if it is to become thoroughly humane and significant. What I have said of William James applies with considerable force to his disciple.

v

In the revulsion that followed America's entry into the war, Randolph Bourne, one of Mr. Dewey's most ardent and talented disciples, found himself bereft of the philosophy which had once seemed all-sufficient; its counsel of adjustment left him rebelliously turning his back on the war-situation and the war-technique. In his recoil, Bourne put his finger upon the shallow side of Mr. Dewey's thinking; and his criticism is all the more adequate and pertinent because it rested on a sympathetic understanding of the instrumentalist philosophy.

"To those of us," he wrote, "who have taken Dewey's philosophy almost as our American religion, it never occurred that values could be subordinated to technique. We were instrumentalist, but we had our private utopias so clearly before our minds that the means fell always into place as contributory. And Dewey, of course, always meant his philosophy, when taken as a philosophy of life, to start with values. But there was always that unhappy ambiguity in his doctrine as to just how values were created, and it became easier and easier to assume that just any growth was justified and almost any activity valuable so long as it achieved its ends. The American, in living out his philosophy, has habitually confused results with product, and been content with getting somewhere without asking too closely whether it was the desirable place to get. . . . You must have your vision, and you must have your technique. The practical effect of Dewey's philosophy has evidently been to develop the sense of the latter at the expense of the former."

Without these superimposed values, the values that arise out of vision, instrumentalism becomes the mere apotheosis of actualities: it is all dressed up, with no place to go. Unfortunately, since the break-up of medieval culture, with such interludes as humanism and romanticism have supplied, men have subordinated the imagination to their interest in practical arrangements and expediences, or they have completely canalized the imagination itself into the practical channels of invention. This has led not alone to the conquest of the physical environment but also to the maceration of human purposes. The more men go on in this way, the farther they go from the domain of the imagination, and the more impossible it becomes for them to recognize the part that vision must play in bringing all their practical activities into a common focus. Their external determinism is only a reflection of their internal impotence: their "it must" can be translated "we can't." As Bourne said, the whole industrial world —and instrumentalism is only its highest conscious expression—has taken values for granted; and the result is that we are the victims of any chance set of values which happens to be left over from the past, or to become the fashion. We are living on fragments of the old cultures, or on abortions of the new, because the energies that should have gone into the imaginative life are balked at the source by the pervasive instrumentalism of the environment.

An instrumental philosophy which was oriented towards a whole life would begin, I think, not by a criticism of obsolete cultural values—which are already criticized by the fact that they are obsolete and inoperative and the possession of a small academic class—it would begin, rather, by a criticism of this one-sided idealization of practical contrivances. We shall not get much nearer a genuine culture by ignoring all the products of the creative imagination, or by palming off our practical instrumentalities—excellent though they are in their place—as their full equivalent. "If your ideal is to be adjustment to the situation," as Bourne well said, "in radiant coöperation with reality, then your success is likely to be just that, and no more. You never transcend anything. . . . Vision must constantly outshoot technique, opportunist efforts usually achieve even less than what obviously seemed possible. An impossibilist *élan* that appeals to desire will often carry farther. A philosophy of adjustment will not even make for adjustment."

Brave words! The pragmatists have been defeated, these last few centuries, because they have not searched for the kingdom, the power, and the glory together, but have sought to achieve power alone; so that the kingdom ceased to be a tangible one, and they knew no glory, except that which flowed out of their pursuit of power. Without vision, the pragmatists perish. And our generation, in particular, who have seen them fall back, one by one, into commercial affairs, into administrative absorption, into a pained abandonment of "reform," into taking whatever fortune thrusts into their laps, into an acquiescence even more pathetic, perhaps, than that of the disabled generation which followed the Civil War—our generation may well doubt the adequacy of their complaisant philosophy. "Things are in the saddle," Emerson said, "and ride mankind." We must overthrow the rider, before we can recover the horse: for otherwise, horse and rider may drive to the devil.

CHAPTER SEVEN

ENVOI

ENVOI

ENTERING our own day, one finds the relations of culture and experience a little difficult to trace out. With the forces that have come over from the past, it is fairly easy to reckon: but how these are being modified or supplanted by new efforts of experience and new stores of culture one cannot with any assurance tell. Is Robert Frost the evening star of New England, or the first streak of a new dawn? Will the Dewey who is struggling to step outside his old preoccupations influence the coming generation, or will the more passive and utilitarian thinker continue to dominate? Will our daily activities center more completely in metropolises, for which the rest of the country serves merely as raw material, or will the politics and economics which produce this state give place to programs of regional development? What is the meaning of Lindsay and Sandburg and Mrs. Mary Austin? What is the promise of regional universities like Nebraska and North Carolina and New Mexico? May we look forward to a steady process of re-settlement; or will the habits of nomadry, expansion, and standardization prevail?

The notion that the forces that are now dominant will inevitably continue and grow stronger will not stand a close examination. Those who take refuge in this comfortable view are merely accepting facts as hopes when they think this would be desirable, or hopes as facts, when they profess that it is unavoidable. The effort of an age may not lead to its prolongation: it may serve to sharpen its antithesis and prepare the way for its own demise. So the stiffening of the old Renaissance motifs in the Eighteenth Century did not lead to their persistence: they formed the thorny nest in which Romanticism was hatched. It was in the decade of Watt's steam engine that Percy's Reliques were published; it was in the decade of the steamboat that Scott published his Waverley novels. Romanticism, for all its superficialities, gave men the liberty to breathe again; out of the clever imitations of Chatterton grew Wordsworth, and out of the meretricious Gothic of Walpole, Hugo and Viollet-le-Duc took possession anew of Notre Dame. I do not say that the Romantic poets changed the course of industrialism; but they altered the mood in which industrialism was received and quickened the recognition of its potentialities for evil, which a blind and complacent utilitarianism might have ignored for generations.

We have seen American culture as formed largely by two events: the breakdown of the medieval synthesis, in the centuries that preceded America's settlement and by the transferal to the new soil of an abstract and fragmentary culture, given definitive form by the Protestants of the Sixteenth Century, by the philosophers and scientists of the Seventeenth, and by the political thinkers of the Eighteenth Century. Faced with the experience of the American wilderness, we sought, in the capacity of pioneers, to find a new basis for culture in the primitive ways of forest and field, in the occupations of hunter, woodman, miner and pastoral nomad: but these occupations, practiced by people who were as much influenced by the idola of utilitarianism as by the deeper effort of the Romantic Movement, did not lead towards a durable culture: the pioneer environment became favorable to an even bleaker preoccupation with the abstractions of matter, money, and political rights. In this situation, the notion of a complete society, carrying on a complete and symmetrical life, tended to disappear from the minds of every one except the disciples of Fourier; with the result that business, technology, and science not merely occupied their legitimate place but took to themselves all that had hitherto belonged to art, religion, and poetry. Positive knowledge and practical action, which are indispensable elements in every culture, became the only living sources of our own; and as the Nineteenth Century wore on, we moved within an ever narrower circle of experience, living mean and illiberal lives.

The moving out of Europe was not merely due to the lure of free land and a multitude of succulent foods: it pointed to cultural vacancy. For three centuries the best minds in Europe had either been trying to get nourishment from the leftovers of classic culture or the Middle Ages, or they had been trying to reach some older source of experience, in order to supplement their bare spiritual fare. Science built up a new conception of the universe, and it endowed its disciples with the power to understand—and frequently to control—external events; but it achieved these results by treating men's central interests and desires as negligible, ignoring the fact that science itself was but a mode of man's activity as a living creature, and that its effort to cancel out the human element was only a very ingenious human expedient. In America, it was easy for an Emerson or a Whitman to see the importance of welding together the interests which science represented, and those which, through the accidents of its historic development, science denied. Turning from a limited European past to a wider heritage, guiding themselves by all the reports of their own day, these poets continued the old voyages of exploration on the plane of the mind, and, seeking passage to India, found themselves coasting along strange shores. None of the fine minds of the Golden Day was afraid to welcome the new forces that were at large in the world. Need I recall that Whitman wrote an apostrophe to the locomotive, that Emerson said a steamship sailing promptly between America and Europe might be as beautiful as a star, and that Thoreau, who loved to hear the wind in the pine needles, listened with equal pleasure to the music of the telegraph wires?

That practical instrumentalities were to be worshiped, never occurred to these writers; but that they added a new and significant element to our culture, which the poet was ready to absorb and include in his report upon the universe, was profoundly true. It is this awareness of new sources of experience that distinguishes the American writers of the Golden Day from their contemporaries in Europe. That the past was merely provisional, and that the future might be formed afresh were two patent generalizations which they drew directly from their environment. These perceptions called, of course, for great works of the imagination; for in proportion as intelligence was dealing more effectually with the instrumentalities of life, it became more necessary for the imagination to project more complete and satisfying ends. The attempt to prefigure in the imagination a culture which should grow out of and refine the experiences the transplanted European encountered on the new soil, mingling the social heritage of the past with the experience of the present, was the great activity of the Golden Day: the essays of Emerson, the poems of Whitman, the solitary musings of Melville all clustered around this central need. None of these men was caught by the dominant abstractions: each saw life whole, and sought a whole life.

We cannot return to the America of the Golden Day, nor keep it fixed in the postures it once naturally assumed; and we should be far from the spirit of Emerson or Whitman if we attempted to do this. But the principal writers of that time are essential links between our own lives and that earlier, that basic, America. In their work, we can see in pristine state the essential characteristics that still lie under

the surface: and from their example, we can more
readily find our own foundations, and make our own
particular point of departure.   In their imagina-
tions, a new world began to form out of the dis-
tracting chaos: wealth was in its place, and science
was in its place, and the deeper life of man began
again to emerge, no longer stunted or frustrated by
the instrumentalities it had conceived and set to
work.   For us who share their vision, a revival of
the moribund, or a relapse into the pragmatic
acquiescence is equally impossible; and we begin again
to dream Thoreau's dream—of what it means to live
a whole human life.

A complete culture leads to the nurture of the
good life; it permits the fullest use, or sublimation,
of man's natural functions and activities.   Confronted by the raw materials of existence, a culture
works them over into new patterns, in which the woof
of reality is crossed by the warp of desire.   Love
is the type of desire in all its modes; and in the
recent emergence of a handful of artists who by the
force of their inner life have seen the inessential and
makeshift character of a large part of the daily
routine, there is perhaps the prophecy of a new
stream of tendency in American life.

Henry Adams, in his Education, observed that the

American artist, in distinction to all the great writers of classic times, seemed scarcely conscious of the power of sex: he was aware of neither a Virgin nor a Venus. In the works of Sherwood Anderson, Edna Millay, Eugene O'Neill, and Waldo Frank this aversion has disappeared: human passion comes back to the scene with almost volcanic exuberance, drawing all the habits and conventionalties and prudences in its wake. It is through brooding over their sexual experience that Mr. Anderson's characters begin to perceive the weaknesses, the limitations, the sordidness of the life about them: they awaken with the eagerness of a new adolescence to discover, like the father in Many Marriages, that what seemed to them "real life," the externalisms, the business arrangements, the neat routine of office and factory, was in fact an unrelated figment, something which drew upon a boyish self that made sandpiles, whittled sticks, or played soldier and wanted to be captain. Whereas the deep and disruptive force that rouses them, and makes beauty credible and desire realizable, is not, as the Gradgrinds would have it, a dream at all, but the prelude to every enduring reality.

Desire is real! Sherwood Anderson's people come to this, as to a final revelation. But if sexual desire,

why not every human desire? In full lust of life
man is not merely a poor creature, wryly adjusting
himself to external circumstances: he is also a
creator, an artist, making circumstances conform to
the aims and necessities he himself freely imposes.
"Sooner throttle a babe in his cradle," wrote William
Blake, "than nurse an unacted desire;" and in the
deep sense of Blake's application, this covers every
aspect of life, since a failure of desire, imagination,
and vision tends to spread over into every activity.
Practical intelligence and a prudent adjustment to
externalities are useful only in a secondary position:
they are but props to straighten the plant when
it begins to grow: at the bottom of it all must be
a soil and a seed, an inner burgeoning, an eagerness
of life. Art in its many forms is a union of imaginative desire, desire sublimated and socialized, with
actuality: without this union, desires become idiotic,
and actualities perhaps even a little more so. It is
not that our instrumental activities are mean: far
from it: but that life is mean when it is entirely absorbed in instrumental activities. Beneath the organized vivacity of our American communities, who
is not aware of a blankness, a sterility, a boredom,
a despair? Their activity, their very lust, is the

galvanic response to an external stimulus, given by
an organism that is dead.

The power to escape from this sinister world can
come only by the double process of encountering
more complete modes of life, and of reformulating
a more vital tissue of ideas and symbols to supplant
those which have led us into the stereotyped interests and actions which we endeavor in vain to identify with a full human existence. We must rectify
the abstract framework of ideas which we have used,
in lieu of a full culture, these last few centuries.
In part, we shall achieve this by a criticism of the
past, which will bring into the foreground those
things that have been left out of the current scheme
of life and thought. Mr. A. N. Whitehead's Science
and the Modern World, and Mr. Victor Branford's
Science and Sanctity are landmarks towards this
new exploration; for they both suggest the ground-
work of a philosophy which shall be oriented as completely towards Life as the dominant thought since
Descartes has been directed towards the Machine.
To take advantage of our experience and our social
heritage and to help in creating this new idolum is
not the smallest adventure our generation may know.
It is more imaginative than the dreams of the transcendentalist, more practical than the work of the

pragmatists, more drastic than the criticisms of the old social revolutionists, and more deeply cultural than all our early attempts to possess the simulacra of culture. It is nothing less than the effort to conceive a new world.

Allons! the road is before us!

THE END